A Journey into Cybersecurity

Mastering Cybersecurity:
Expert Insights and Best Practices

Cameron Brooks

Table of Contents

CHAPTER XI: Regulatory Compliance and Legal Considerations 115

CHAPTER XII: Building a Cybersecurity Culture 124

CONCLUSION 134

INTRODUCTION

The importance of cybersecurity has risen to new heights in the connected digital world of today. New technologies are developed daily, changing how we work, communicate, and conduct business. However, these developments also bring a wide range of cyber threats and vulnerabilities that are constantly expanding and might seriously disrupt our lives and the operations of our businesses.

"A Journey into Cybersecurity: Mastering Cybersecurity - Expert Insights and Best Practices" is your comprehensive guide to navigating this complex landscape. In this book, we explore the key ideas, tactics, and resources that enable individuals and organizations to protect their digital assets and privacy effectively. Whether you're an IT professional, a business owner, or an individual trying to improve your digital security, this book delivers expert insights and actionable best practices that will assist you stay one step ahead of cyber threats.

Cybersecurity is becoming crucial for anyone who interacts with the digital world, not only technology experts. Securing sensitive data, networks, and systems is now everyone's top priority, from the smallest startups to the biggest corporations, from desktop PCs to networked smart gadgets. Neglecting cybersecurity can have adverse effects on reputation, customer trust, and legal issues, in addition to monetary losses.

We'll embark on a journey through the complex world of cybersecurity on the following pages. We aim to give you a thorough grasp of the core ideas, tactics, and procedures supporting a solid cybersecurity posture.

From the basics of cybersecurity to cutting-edge trends, we've meticulously curated this book to provide valuable insights for individuals at all levels of expertise.

Each chapter focuses on a different area of cybersecurity, providing theoretical explanations, instances from the real world, and helpful advice. We'll delve into the numerous threat environments that people and organizations must contend with, examine the fundamental notions that serve as the cornerstone of effective cybersecurity measures, and walk you through applying best practices that reduce risks and strengthen defenses.

This book is your essential companion whether you're looking to protect your own devices, improve the cybersecurity standards at your company, or learn more about the rapidly changing cybersecurity environment. As we journey through the intricacies of cybersecurity together, you'll be empowered to navigate the digital realm with confidence and mastery.

So, let's start this educational journey into the world of cybersecurity, where professional insights and best practices are waiting to improve your knowledge of digital security.

CHAPTER I

Understanding Cybersecurity Basics

What is Cybersecurity?

In today's hyper-connected world, where information flows seamlessly across virtual networks, the concept of cybersecurity has risen to paramount importance. Cybersecurity refers to protecting digital systems, networks, devices, and data from unauthorized access, cyberattacks, and potential damage. Its significance cannot be overstated, as our digital landscape is rife with opportunities and vulnerabilities that demand constant vigilance and robust defenses.

At its core, cybersecurity encompasses a wide array of strategies, technologies, and practices to maintain digital assets' confidentiality, integrity, and availability. Confidentiality ensures that sensitive information is accessible only to authorized individuals or entities. Integrity entails safeguarding data from unauthorized modifications or tampering, while availability ensures authorized users can access information and services when needed. These three pillars, often called the CIA triad, form the bedrock upon which cybersecurity strategies are built.

One of the critical challenges in cybersecurity is the evolving nature of cyber threats. The strategies and techniques used by malicious actors also advance with technology. Cyberattacks come in various forms, ranging from well-known types such as phishing, malware, and ransomware to more sophisticated attacks like zero-day exploits and advanced persistent threats (APTs). Phishing, for instance, involves tricking individuals into revealing sensitive details or clicking on malicious links, while malware encompasses a range of malicious software designed to infiltrate and compromise systems.

To counteract these threats, cybersecurity professionals employ a multi-faceted approach known as "defense in depth." This strategy involves implementing multiple layers of security controls to create a comprehensive and interconnected defense system. Firewalls, intrusion detection systems, encryption, and access controls are among the many tools utilized in this approach. By establishing redundant layers of protection, organizations can mitigate the impact of potential breaches and ensure that a single vulnerability does not lead to a catastrophic compromise.

Another critical aspect of cybersecurity is user awareness and training. Human behavior is frequently the weakest link within the security chain. Social engineering attacks, such as spear phishing, exploit psychological and emotional triggers to manipulate individuals into divulging confidential information. To address this vulnerability, educating users about common attack techniques, fostering a cautious attitude toward unsolicited communications, and promoting good password hygiene are essential components of a strong cybersecurity culture.

Endpoint security is another focal point in the cybersecurity landscape. Endpoints, which include devices like computers, smartphones, and tablets, are often targeted by cybercriminals as entry points into larger systems. Antivirus software, intrusion prevention systems, and endpoint detection and response (EDR) tools are deployed to safeguard these devices and detect malicious activities in real-time.

The shift towards cloud computing has introduced a new dimension to cybersecurity challenges in recent years. Cloud services offer convenience and scalability but require careful consideration of shared responsibility. Cloud providers are responsible for protecting the underlying infrastructure, while customers must ensure the security of their data and applications. This shared model necessitates a clear understanding of roles and responsibilities to avoid potential gaps in security coverage.

As the digital landscape evolves, so does the cybersecurity field. Emerging technologies like the artificial intelligence and machine learning are being harnessed to enhance threat detection and response capabilities. The Internet of Things (IoT) devices proliferation brings with it new vectors of attack and demands innovative security solutions. Moreover, the dawn of quantum computing poses opportunities and challenges, potentially rendering current encryption methods obsolete while offering new avenues for securing data.

In conclusion, cybersecurity is a crucial bulwark in an increasingly digital world. Its role extends far beyond the realm of technology, encompassing economic stability, national security, and personal privacy. By adhering to the principles of confidentiality, integrity, and availability, adopting a multi-layered defense, and fostering a culture of awareness, individuals and organizations can fortify their digital defenses and navigate the intricate landscape of cybersecurity with resilience and confidence. The ongoing pursuit of cybersecurity excellence is not merely a technical endeavor; it's a commitment to safeguarding the very fabric of our interconnected society.

Types of Cyber Threats and Attacks

In the modern digital age, where interconnected systems and networks have become the backbone of nearly every facet of society, the prevalence and sophistication of cyber threats and attacks have risen exponentially. These digital intrusions, ranging from data breaches to disruptive attacks on critical infrastructure, pose significant challenges to individuals, businesses, and governments. Understanding the multitude of cyber threats is paramount in devising effective defense strategies. This section delves into the diverse categories of cyber threats and attacks, exploring their methodologies, motivations, real-world examples, and the importance of cybersecurity preparedness.

Malware, short for malicious software, represents one of the most pervasive and versatile threats in the digital realm. It encompasses a range of malicious programs that aim to infiltrate systems, compromise data, and wreak havoc. Viruses, for instance, attach themselves to legitimate files and replicate when the infected file is executed, spreading the malware further. Worms, on the other hand, are self-replicating programs that exploit vulnerabilities to spread across networks. Trojans disguise themselves as legitimate software but harbor malicious intent, often providing attackers with unauthorized access to systems. Ransomware encrypts data of the victims and demands a ransom for its release, while spyware silently monitors and collects user data without consent. The dynamic nature of malware underscores the need for robust cybersecurity measures to detect, prevent, and mitigate its impact.

Phishing attacks capitalize on human psychology and social engineering to deceive individuals into divulging sensitive information or performing actions compromising security. Cybercriminals impersonate trusted entities, often through well-crafted emails or websites, to manipulate recipients into providing credentials, financial information, or access to confidential systems. Spear phishing narrows the target to specific individuals or organizations, allowing attackers to tailor messages that appear authentic and relevant to their recipients.

Whaling, a variant of spear phishing, targets high-profile individuals, such as executives, leveraging their influence to gain unauthorized access to critical systems. The success of phishing attacks highlights the importance of user education and cybersecurity awareness to counter this insidious threat.

Denial of Service (DoS) attacks flood target systems, such as websites or networks, with excessive traffic, overwhelming their resources and rendering them inaccessible to legitimate users. Distributed Denial of Service (DDoS) attacks amplify this tactic by coordinating traffic from multiple sources, often through botnets, to orchestrate a more massive assault. The primary objective of DoS and DDoS attacks is to disrupt services, causing operational and financial losses and tarnishing an organization's reputation. Mitigating these attacks requires robust network infrastructure, real-time monitoring, and rapid response capabilities.

Unlike external attacks, insider threats stem from individuals within an organization who exploit their authorized access for malicious purposes. These individuals might have legitimate access to sensitive data, networks, or systems, making detecting their actions challenging. Insider threats can be accidental, as employees inadvertently compromise security, or intentional, when individuals misuse their privileges for personal gain or to damage the organization. Detecting and mitigating insider threats requires a combination of user behavior analytics, access controls, and a strong organizational culture that values cybersecurity ethics.

Well-funded and organized adversaries, such as nation-states or corporate espionage groups orchestrate Advanced Persistent Threats (APTs). These attacks are characterized by their sophisticated planning, long-term execution, and stealthy approach. To infiltrate and compromise high-value targets, APTs combine multiple attack vectors, including malware, social engineering, and zero-day vulnerabilities. Once inside, attackers maintain persistent access to the target's network, exfiltrating valuable data over extended periods. The stealth and patience displayed by APTs highlight the importance of regular monitoring, threat intelligence, and timely incident response.

Man-in-the-Middle (MitM) attacks involve intercepting and altering communication between two parties, unbeknownst to either side. Attackers position themselves between the sender and receiver, capturing and potentially modifying data transmitted between them. These attacks often occur on unsecured public Wi-Fi networks, where cybercriminals exploit vulnerabilities to intercept sensitive information, such as financial details or login credentials. MitM attacks underscore the importance of using secure and encrypted communication channels, particularly when accessing public networks.

Zero-day exploits target software vulnerabilities that vendors are unaware of, allowing attackers to use these flaws before patches are developed and distributed. Hackers leverage these unknown vulnerabilities to compromise systems, often causing significant damage or exfiltrating sensitive data. The challenge with zero-day exploits is that organizations must respond quickly to develop and deploy patches once the vulnerability is discovered, minimizing the risk of exploitation. Robust patch management, vulnerability assessments, and threat intelligence are critical in mitigating zero-day threats.

Social engineering attacks manipulate human psychology and behavior to deceive individuals into divulging confidential information, performing actions that compromise security, or inadvertently aiding attackers. Pretexting involves creating a fabricated scenario to elicit information from the target, while baiting entices victims to download malware by offering something appealing, such as a free software download. As previously discussed, phishing is a common social engineering tactic that targets a wide range of individuals and organizations. The success of social engineering attacks hinges on exploiting human vulnerability, making cybersecurity awareness training and education vital in countering these threats.

Supply chain attacks target vulnerabilities within third-party vendors or partners accessing an organization's systems or networks. Cybercriminals compromise these vendors to gain unauthorized access or spread malware to the target organization. Attackers exploit the trust established between the target and the vendor to infiltrate systems, exfiltrate data, or distribute malicious code. Recent high-profile incidents have demonstrated the potential impact of supply chain attacks, emphasizing the importance of assessing the security practices of third-party partners and implementing robust access controls.

The Internet of Things (IoT) devices rapid proliferation introduces new attack vectors, as these devices often lack robust security features. IoT attacks exploit vulnerabilities in interconnected devices, ranging from smart home devices to critical infrastructure components. Compromised IoT devices can serve as entry points to more extensive networks, disrupting services, compromising data, or even facilitating large-scale attacks. Securing the IoT ecosystem requires stringent security measures, including device authentication, encryption, and regular updates.

Ransomware attacks encrypt an organization's data, rendering it inaccessible, and demand a ransom, usually in cryptocurrency, for the decryption key. The notorious WannaCry attack in 2017 affected hundreds of thousands of computers worldwide, highlighting the global impact of ransomware. These attacks can cause significant disruption, financial losses, and damage to an organization's reputation. Preventing ransomware requires a multi-layered approach, including regular backups, robust security practices, and employee education to recognize potential threats.

As cryptocurrencies gain prominence, cybercriminals have turned to cryptojacking, a technique that hijacks victims' computing resources to mine cryptocurrencies without their consent. Cryptojacking strains systems, slows down performance, and drains energy resources. Cybercriminals often spread cryptojacking malware through malicious websites, compromised ads, or even infected IoT devices. Preventing cryptojacking necessitates robust endpoint security, ad-blockers, and vigilant monitoring for unusual resource consumption. State-sponsored attacks involve governments or government-backed entities targeting other nations' critical infrastructure, sensitive data, or military systems. These attacks serve political, economic, or strategic objectives, often involving significant resources and advanced techniques. The Stuxnet worm, broadly believed to be a product of a state-sponsored attack, targeted Iran's nuclear facilities, illustrating the potential impact of these intrusions on global security. State- sponsored attacks pose unique challenges due to their geopolitical implications, necessitating strong international cooperation and robust cybersecurity measures.

In conclusion, cyber threats' intricate and constantly evolving landscape underscores the critical need for proactive cybersecurity measures in the digital age. From malware and phishing to APTs and state-sponsored attacks, the multitude of threat vectors demands a comprehensive approach that includes continuous monitoring, threat intelligence, education, and incident response planning. Organizations and individuals must be aware of their potential risks and vulnerabilities, utilizing a combination of technological solutions, best practices, and collaboration to fortify their digital defenses. In the realm of cybersecurity, vigilance, adaptability, and preparedness are paramount in navigating the multifaceted world of cyber threats and attacks.

The Evolution of Cybersecurity Landscape

In the contemporary digital age, the evolution of the cybersecurity landscape has mirrored the rapid advancement of technology and the intricate challenges posed by an interconnected world. As technology has woven itself into the fabric of modern society, the need to protect the digital infrastructure from an array of threats has spurred the growth of cybersecurity into a multidimensional and dynamic field. This section delves into the historical progression of the cybersecurity landscape, tracing its evolution from its roots to the complexities of the present day, examining key milestones, transformative developments, emerging threats, and the enduring significance of staying ahead in the relentless quest to safeguard digital assets.

The origins of the cybersecurity landscape can be traced back to the early days of computing when the digital landscape was in its infancy. In the 1970s and 1980s, computer security focused on safeguarding physical access to mainframe computers and ensuring data integrity. The introduction of passwords and access controls marked the initial steps towards creating a secure computing environment. However, these early security measures were often limited to protecting individual systems, with little consideration for the broader interconnected nature of emerging networks.

As the 1990s dawned and the world began to witness the emergence of the internet, the cybersecurity landscape underwent a seismic shift. The need to secure data transmissions and protect against unauthorized access became evident with the rapid expansion of networks. Firewalls and intrusion detection systems emerged as the first line of defense against external threats. Yet, the advent of viruses, worms, and other malware highlighted the vulnerabilities within software and operating systems. The "ILOVEYOU" virus of 2000 and the Code Red worm of 2001 exposed the potential for widespread disruption, propelling the development of more sophisticated antivirus software and security protocols.

The early 2000s marked a transition from disruptive attacks to data breaches, as cybercriminals began targeting personal and financial information for financial gain. High-profile breaches, such as the Heartland Payment Systems breach in 2008, emphasized the value of customer data to attackers. In response, regulatory frameworks like the Payment Card Industry Data Security Standard (PCI DSS) emerged to enforce security standards for handling payment card information. This era witnessed the maturation of encryption techniques and the emergence of secure socket layer (SSL) protocols, aimed at protecting data as it traversed the digital landscape.

By the mid-2010s, a paradigm shift was underway in the realm of cyberattacks. Advanced persistent threats (APTs) emerged as a dominant force, reflecting a convergence of tactics that allowed attackers to infiltrate and compromise high-value targets. Stuxnet, a complex worm discovered in 2010, epitomized the fusion of digital and physical threats by targeting industrial control systems. APTs demonstrated unprecedented persistence, challenging traditional notions of threat response and necessitating threat intelligence integration, real-time monitoring, and sophisticated incident response strategies.

The proliferation of smartphones and the rise of the Internet of Things (IoT) introduced new dimensions to cybersecurity. Mobile devices, becoming increasingly integral to daily life, presented fresh opportunities for cybercriminals to exploit vulnerabilities and access sensitive information. The emergence of botnets, such as the Mirai botnet in 2016, illustrated the potential of IoT devices as vectors for distributed denial of service (DDoS) attacks. The challenges these interconnected ecosystems pose underscored the need for robust security mechanisms and the implementation of security-by-design principles.

In the latter half of the 2010s, the landscape witnessed the ascendancy of ransomware as a lucrative avenue for cybercriminals. Attacks like WannaCry in 2017 exposed the vulnerabilities of organizations and individuals alike, encrypting data and demanding ransom payments for decryption keys. Moreover, nation-state attacks began to blur the lines between cyber espionage and disruption. The NotPetya attack of the same year, attributed to state- sponsored actors, showcased the potential for cyber operations to have far-reaching economic and geopolitical ramifications. These incidents emphasized the necessity of robust incident response planning, international cooperation, and proactive defense strategies.

The cybersecurity landscape has evolved into an intricate and multifaceted domain in the modern era. Cybercriminals leverage advanced techniques, often harnessing artificial intelligence and machine learning to automate attacks and evade traditional defense mechanisms. Nation-states, meanwhile, engage in cyber operations that transcend mere technical actions, engendering geopolitical implications and economic consequences. The SolarWinds supply chain attack in 2020, attributed to state-sponsored actors, highlighted the potential impact of targeting trusted software vendors, unveiling the depth of the challenges that modern cybersecurity confronts.

As the cybersecurity landscape evolves, the trajectory remains uncertain. Emerging technologies, including quantum computing and 5G networks, promise both advancements and vulnerabilities that demand innovative solutions. The proliferation of smart cities, artificial intelligence, and autonomous systems adds complexity to the cybersecurity paradigm. Ensuring the security of these intricate ecosystems requires interdisciplinary collaboration, dynamic threat modeling, and a commitment to staying ahead of emerging threats.

In conclusion, the journey of the cybersecurity landscape is an ongoing saga that mirrors the relentless pace of technological advancement. From rudimentary access controls to the intricacies of APTs and nation-state operations, the field has evolved from mitigating isolated incidents to navigating a complex and ever-expanding digital frontier. As cyberspace grows, the imperative to secure digital assets against various threats remains unwavering. Cybersecurity guardians must remain vigilant, adaptive, and innovative in safeguarding the digital realm. Collaboration, continuous education, and proactive defense will continue to be the guiding beacons in a landscape characterized by unceasing change and the perpetual quest for resilience in the face of evolving challenges.

CHAPTER II

Key Cybersecurity Principles

Confidentiality, Integrity, and Availability (CIA Triad)

In the intricate web of cybersecurity, the principles of Confidentiality, Integrity, and Availability, collectively known as the CIA Triad, stand as foundational pillars that underpin the design, implementation, and evaluation of robust security measures. As technology continues to infiltrate every facet of our lives, safeguarding digital assets has become paramount, and the CIA Triad provides a framework to achieve this by addressing the fundamental aspects of data protection and system functionality.

Confidentiality revolves around ensuring that sensitive information remains accessible only to authorized individuals or entities. Maintaining confidentiality has become a complex endeavor in an era marked by information sharing and digital interconnectedness. From personal data and trade secrets to medical records and financial information, a vast array of information requires protection from prying eyes. Encryption plays a pivotal role in achieving confidentiality. It transforms data into an unreadable format unless decrypted with the appropriate key, ensuring that they cannot decipher its contents even if unauthorized individuals gain access to the data.

Integrity focuses on safeguarding the accuracy and trustworthiness of data. In a world where digital manipulations can occur silently and swiftly, ensuring that information remains unaltered is crucial. The integrity principle guarantees that data is protected from unauthorized modifications, whether accidental or malicious. Hash functions and digital signatures are often employed to achieve data integrity. Hash functions generate unique strings of characters based on data inputs, allowing for quick verification of data authenticity. Digital signatures provide cryptographic proof of the origin and unchanged state of data, ensuring that recipients can trust the validity of the information they receive.

Availability ensures that authorized users can access information and services when needed. Uninterrupted access is paramount, whether it's an individual accessing their emails, an organization processing transactions, or a nation's critical infrastructure. Cyberattacks that disrupt availability, such as Distributed Denial of Service (DDoS) attacks, seek to overwhelm systems and render them inaccessible. Robust redundancy, failover mechanisms, and load balancing are implemented to maintain availability. Additionally, disaster recovery and business continuity plans are vital to ensuring that essential services can be restored swiftly in the face of unexpected disruptions.

The CIA Triad is not a set of isolated principles; they often intersect and require careful balancing. For example, strong encryption that ensures confidentiality might hinder availability if decryption processes are slow or resource-intensive. Similarly, rigorous access controls that enhance confidentiality could inadvertently compromise data integrity if unauthorized parties make changes. This delicate interplay requires a nuanced approach to cybersecurity, where a comprehensive understanding of an organization's unique needs guides the implementation of measures that uphold all three principles simultaneously.

The modern cybersecurity landscape poses challenges to the CIA Triad. As organizations embrace remote work and cloud computing, data is accessed from diverse locations and devices, increasing the potential attack surface. Balancing accessibility and security becomes more intricate. Additionally, the rise of state-sponsored cyber operations and advanced persistent threats have blurred the lines between traditional confidentiality, integrity, and availability concepts. Attackers seek not only to breach systems but also to manipulate or undermine data to achieve their goals.

The CIA Triad, while foundational, has evolved to include additional attributes such as authenticity, accountability, and non-repudiation. Authenticity ensures that data originates from a genuine source, reducing the risk of receiving misleading or deceptive information. Accountability involves tracing actions back to responsible parties, deterring malicious activities. Non-repudiation prevents individuals from denying their actions, ensuring that there is evidence to establish their occurrence once an action is performed.

In conclusion, in an era where data breaches and cyberattacks dominate headlines, the CIA Triad stands as a guiding light in the complex realm of cybersecurity. These principles transcend mere technical considerations; they encompass ethics, law, and the very fabric of trust upon which the digital world rests. Striving for confidentiality, integrity, and availability requires a holistic approach that considers not only technology but also human behavior, regulatory compliance, and the constantly evolving threat landscape. As individuals, organizations, and nations navigate the ever-expanding digital frontier, the CIA Triad provides a compass, leading toward a safer and more secure cyber ecosystem.

Defense in Depth Strategy

In the relentless and evolving cybersecurity landscape, where threats loom and attacks grow increasingly sophisticated, the Defense in Depth strategy has emerged as a critical approach to safeguarding digital assets. As organizations and individuals embrace technology for enhanced productivity and connectivity, the need for comprehensive protection has never been greater. The Defense in Depth strategy offers a multi-layered, holistic approach that recognizes the inevitability of breaches and seeks to minimize their impact through proactive and reactive measures.

The Defense in Depth strategy is about creating a fortified architecture employing multiple security control layers. These layers function in tandem, each adding a unique defense dimension to the overall security posture. This approach mirrors the layers of an onion, where even if one layer is compromised, additional barriers are in place to thwart attackers' progress. Each layer aims to mitigate risks associated with specific threats and vulnerabilities, ultimately contributing to a more resilient system.

The outermost layer of the Defense in Depth strategy focuses on physical security measures. Access controls, surveillance, and security personnel are deployed to hinder unauthorized physical access to facilities and equipment. This layer is a fundamental barrier against physical threats such as theft, tampering, and espionage. While it may seem distant from the digital realm, physical security is the foundation upon which the rest of the strategy is built, emphasizing that cybersecurity extends beyond lines of code.

Perimeter security establishes the first line of defense against cyber threats. Firewalls, intrusion detection systems (IDS), as well as intrusion prevention systems (IPS) are pivotal in this layer. Firewalls act as gatekeepers, inspecting incoming and outgoing network traffic and allowing or blocking based on predefined rules. IDS and IPS monitor network activities for suspicious behavior, alerting administrators to potential breaches. By analyzing traffic patterns and identifying anomalies, these controls serve as sentinels guarding the entry points of digital systems.

Within the network layer, the focus shifts to internal segmentation and isolation. Network segmentation entails dividing a network into smaller, isolated segments, reducing the potential impact of breaches. This technique restricts lateral movement for attackers, preventing them from quickly traversing the network once inside. Additionally, virtual local area networks (VLANs) and network access controls (NAC) ensure that only authorized users and devices can access specific network parts, minimizing the attack surface.

Endpoints—devices like computers, smartphones, and tablets—represent access points and potential vulnerabilities. Endpoint security encompasses antivirus and anti-malware software, endpoint detection and response (EDR) solutions, and mobile device management (MDM) tools. These controls safeguard against malicious software and unauthorized access, reducing the likelihood of attacks originating from compromised devices.

The heart of the Defense in Depth strategy lies in protecting the data itself. Data security involves encryption, ensuring that even if attackers breach other layers, the data they access remains unintelligible without the decryption key. Encryption can be utilized for data at rest (stored data), data in transit (data being transmitted between systems), and data in use (data actively processed by applications). Encryption algorithms and protocols provide an additional defense against data breaches and unauthorized access.

Applications, often the primary interface between users and systems, are a crucial focus of the Defense in Depth strategy. Application security involves secure coding practices, vulnerability assessments, and penetration testing. Secure development lifecycles (SDLC) are implemented to ensure that software is designed, coded, and tested with security in mind from the outset. Web application firewalls (WAFs) and runtime application self-protection (RASP) technologies monitor and protect applications from malicious activities and attacks.

The human factor is a vital element of the Defense in Depth strategy. Through social engineering attacks or poor security hygiene, users, whether employees or individuals, may unintentionally turn into weak links in the security chain. User awareness and training programs educate individuals about cybersecurity best practices, fostering a security-conscious culture. Organizations bolster their overall security posture by empowering users to determine and respond to potential threats.

Even with robust preventive measures, breaches may still occur. The incident response layer focuses on rapid detection, containment, mitigation, and recovery. Incident response plans (IRPs) outline steps to be taken when a breach occurs, minimizing the damage and downtime. Cybersecurity professionals and response teams are trained to address breaches swiftly, analyze the extent of compromise, and facilitate recovery while minimizing disruption.

In conclusion, the Defense in Depth strategy is not a single solution but an orchestration of protective layers working together to create a comprehensive and resilient security posture. As cyber threats evolve, the strategy's adaptability remains its greatest strength. Organizations must continually assess and update their defenses to address new vulnerabilities and attack vectors. By embracing a holistic approach that acknowledges the inevitability of breaches and aims to mitigate their impact, the Defense in Depth strategy equips individuals and organizations with a formidable arsenal to navigate the complex cyber battleground.

Least Privilege and Role-Based Access Control

In the intricate realm of cybersecurity, where the battle between defenders and adversaries rages, the principles of Least Privilege (LP) and Role-Based Access Control (RBAC) emerge as vital tools in safeguarding digital assets. These principles address a fundamental challenge: granting users the required access to perform their tasks while minimizing the potential for unauthorized actions and data breaches. In a world where interconnected systems abound and cyber threats continually evolve, LP and RBAC offer a strategic approach to secure authorization that champions functionality and security.

At the heart of the Least Privilege principle lies the philosophy that users should be granted the lowest level of access necessary to perform their duties. This means that individuals are given access only to the essential resources and data for their specific roles. Restricting access beyond what is necessary significantly reduces the possible damage caused by a compromised account or human error. Essentially, the principle of Least Privilege follows the adage "less is more" regarding user access.

The benefits of adopting the Least Privilege principle are numerous and profound. By adhering to this principle, organizations minimize the potential attack surface available to malicious actors. Even if an attacker obtain an access to a user's credentials, their ability to move laterally within the network and access critical data is constrained. This limitation hampers the ability of attackers to escalate privileges, thereby thwarting their attempts to exploit vulnerabilities. Furthermore, in the event of an insider threat or accidental data exposure, the principle of Least Privilege minimizes the potential impact and damage.

Implementing the principle of Least Privilege has its challenges. Balancing security with the need for productivity requires careful consideration. Overly restrictive access can impede workflow and frustrate users, potentially leading to workarounds that undermine security measures. Careful planning and a deep understanding of users' roles and responsibilities are essential to finding the right balance. Moreover, managing access rights across a complex network can be labor-intensive. However, modern identity and access management (IAM) solutions provide automation and centralized control, easing the administrative burden.

Role-Based Access Control (RBAC) builds upon the foundation of the Least Privilege principle by organizing users into roles and assigning permissions based on those roles. In RBAC, access rights are tied to specific job functions or responsibilities rather than individual users. This creates a structured access management approach, ensuring permissions are consistent, transparent, and aligned with organizational roles.

RBAC introduces a new layer of granularity to access control. By mapping permissions to roles, RBAC enables organizations to define fine-grained access based on specific tasks and responsibilities. This contrasts with the binary approach of traditional access control, which often only distinguishes between "allowed" and "not allowed." Additionally, as organizations grow and roles evolve, RBAC offers scalability. Instead of manually adjusting permissions for each user, changes can be made at the role level, streamlining administration and reducing the risk of errors.

The successful implementation of RBAC requires a systematic approach. The first step is to define and categorize roles based on job functions and responsibilities. Next, permissions are assigned to each role, reflecting the tasks associated with that role. This mapping can be done through manual assessment or automated tools that analyze historical user behavior. As user roles evolve, the RBAC model ensures that permissions are adjusted accordingly, minimizing the risk of access creep and ensuring ongoing alignment between user responsibilities and permissions.

The Least Privilege and Role-Based Access Control principles are not mutually exclusive; they complement and reinforce each other. The structured approach of RBAC aids in the practical implementation of Least Privilege. By organizing users into roles and assigning permissions based on their responsibilities, RBAC inherently limits access to what is necessary for the user's function. Conversely, Least Privilege bolsters RBAC by reinforcing the need for minimal access, discouraging the assignment of unnecessary permissions to roles.

The advent of cloud computing, mobile devices, and the Internet of Things (IoT) has introduced new dimensions to access control challenges. Users can access resources from various locations and devices, requiring dynamic and context-aware authorization. Advanced technologies such as contextual access management and adaptive authentication are emerging to address these complexities. These technologies leverage user behavior patterns, device information, and contextual data to make real-time access decisions that align with Least Privilege and RBAC principles.

In conclusion, in the multifaceted landscape of cybersecurity, where unauthorized access and data breaches lurk at every digital corner, the principles of Least Privilege and Role-Based Access Control shine as guiding lights. These principles are not just technical strategies; they reflect a philosophy that champions security without sacrificing productivity. By adopting the disciplined approach of granting only the necessary access and organizing permissions based on roles, organizations and individuals can forge a secure path through the digital wilderness, safeguarding data, maintaining compliance, and mitigating risks in a world of perpetual cyber challenges.

Patch Management and Software Updates

In the ever-evolving landscape of cybersecurity, where threats and vulnerabilities continue to increase, patch management and software updates have emerged as indispensable practices for maintaining the robustness of digital systems. As technology advances at a quick pace, so too does the sophistication of cyberattacks. Cybercriminals exploit vulnerabilities in software to breach systems, exfiltrate sensitive data, and wreak havoc. The critical role of patch management and software updates in mitigating these risks cannot be overstated. These practices represent a dynamic and ongoing effort to fortify the digital fortress, ensuring that software remains resilient, secure, and adaptive to the ever-changing threat landscape.

Software vulnerabilities are an inherent part of the digital landscape. As software is developed and deployed, coding errors, design flaws, and unforeseen interactions can create openings for malicious actors to exploit. Cybercriminals quickly capitalize on these vulnerabilities, crafting attacks that target unpatched systems. The challenge lies not only in identifying vulnerabilities but also in addressing them timely and effectively.

Patch management is the systematic process of identifying, evaluating, testing, and applying updates or patches to software systems. Patches are designed to correct identified vulnerabilities, improve software functionality, and address performance issues. The aim of patch management is twofold: to reduce the window of attackers chances to exploit vulnerabilities and to maintain the overall health and integrity of software.

Software updates encompass a broader scope than patches, as they can include new features, bug fixes, performance enhancements, and security updates. Regular software updates ensure that software remains compatible with evolving technologies and user requirements. These updates reflect the ongoing commitment of software developers to deliver the best possible user experience while addressing security concerns.

The timely application of patches and software updates is crucial to effective cybersecurity. The "zero-day" period is the time frame that exists between the identification of a vulnerability and the release of a patch to address it. During this time, systems are most vulnerable, as attackers can exploit the vulnerability before a fix is available. Organizations must race against the clock to deploy patches and updates swiftly to reduce this exposure.

While patch management and software updates are essential, they are not without challenges. The complexity of modern software ecosystems, particularly in large organizations, can make it challenging to track and manage all deployed software instances. The installation of patches and updates must be balanced, ensuring that the updates are stable and compatible with existing systems. Incompatibilities can lead to downtime, data loss, and operational disruptions.

Automation has appeared as a valuable tool in the realm of patch management and software updates. Automated systems can scan networks for vulnerabilities, prioritize patches based on severity, and deploy updates across multiple systems simultaneously. However, while automation can enhance efficiency, it must be carefully managed to prevent unintended consequences, such as deploying updates without proper testing or disrupting critical processes.

Effective patch management requires a systematic approach combining technical expertise and strategic planning. Organizations should establish a patch management policy that outlines procedures for identifying, testing, approving, and deploying patches. A dedicated team or individual responsible for overseeing patch management ensures accountability and consistency. Regular penetration testing and vulnerability assessments help identify vulnerabilities that may require patching.

Users play a pivotal role in the success of patch management and software updates. Educating users about the importance of updates, the risks of delaying patches, and how to recognize legitimate update prompts versus phishing attempts is essential. Creating a culture of cybersecurity awareness encourages users to actively participate in maintaining the security of the digital ecosystem.

As technology evolves, so too will the methods of software exploitation. Threats will become more sophisticated, potentially targeting vulnerabilities that traditional patch management approaches may not effectively address. Machine learning and artificial intelligence could play a role in identifying and mitigating vulnerabilities more efficiently. Moreover, the rise of interconnected devices in the Internet of Things (IoT) introduces new challenges in managing updates across diverse platforms.

In conclusion, patch management and software updates represent a never-ending journey in pursuing cybersecurity excellence. The digital landscape is marked by constant change, and as software evolves, so do the vulnerabilities it may introduce. Organizations and individuals must embrace a proactive and holistic approach, acknowledging that security is not a destination but an ongoing process. By prioritizing timely updates, establishing robust patch management procedures, and fostering a culture of vigilance, we can collectively navigate the dynamic cyber terrain, bolster our digital defenses, and build a more secure and resilient digital future.

CHAPTER III

The Human Factor in Cybersecurity

Social Engineering Attacks (Phishing, Spear Phishing, etc.)

Social engineering attacks are a formidable and insidious adversary in the ever-evolving landscape of cybersecurity threats. Rooted in the manipulation of human psychology, these attacks exploit the innate vulnerabilities of human nature to breach digital defenses. From phishing and spear phishing to pretexting and baiting, social engineering attacks have repeatedly proven that technological fortifications alone are insufficient to counter the allure of a well-crafted deception. This section delves into the intricate world of social engineering attacks, dissecting their methodologies, exploring real-world examples, analyzing their impact on individuals and organizations, and highlighting the indispensable role of education and awareness in mitigating these threats.

Social engineering attacks are a class of cyber threats that rely on manipulating human behavior to compromise security. These attacks aim to exploit the inherent trust, curiosity, and even fear that characterize human interactions. Cybercriminals orchestrate these attacks by meticulously crafting scenarios that induce targets to divulge sensitive information, perform actions that compromise security, or inadvertently open the door to malicious activities. Unlike traditional technical exploits that target software vulnerabilities, social engineering exploits the human element, making it a potent tool for adversaries.

Phishing attacks are perhaps the most recognizable form of social engineering. Cybercriminals masquerade as legitimate entities, often through emails or messages, and trick recipients into divulging sensitive information such as passwords, credit card details, or personal information. These messages are designed to trigger urgency or fear, enticing recipients to act impulsively. The prolific nature of phishing campaigns is evidenced by the countless malicious emails that flood inboxes, impersonating banks, social media platforms, and even trusted service providers. The success of phishing attacks hinges on luring unsuspecting victims into divulging valuable data, often leading to identity theft, financial loss, and compromised accounts.

Spear phishing takes the art of deception a step further by tailoring attacks to specific individuals or organizations. Attackers gather information from various sources, such as social media profiles or leaked databases, to personalize their messages and increase their credibility. By referencing personal details or using familiar context, spear phishers create an illusion of legitimacy, making recipients more likely to engage. A prominent example is the 2016 attack on John Podesta, the chairman of Hillary Clinton's presidential campaign, where a seemingly innocuous spear phishing email led to the compromise of sensitive campaign information. The targeted nature of spear phishing underscores the need for cautious online behavior and robust security measures.

Pretexting involves the creation of a fabricated scenario or pretext to elicit information from targets. Attackers assume a false identity, often impersonating authoritative figures or service providers, and use persuasive narratives to manipulate victims into sharing sensitive data. These scenarios could involve urgent requests for account verification, financial assistance, or personal information updates. Pretexting exploits the natural human tendency to be helpful and compliant, leading victims to expose valuable information unwittingly. This form of manipulation has been employed in scenarios ranging from gaining unauthorized access to secure facilities to extracting confidential corporate data.

Baiting attacks capitalize on human curiosity or desire for gain. Attackers offer enticing baits, such as free software downloads, music, or movies, to lure victims into downloading malware-infected files. The allure of free or exclusive content can bypass rational judgment, enticing victims to perform actions that compromise their security. Baiting can take various forms, from physical media like infected USB drives left in conspicuous places to online downloads promising desirable content. The Stuxnet worm, for example, was introduced through a baiting attack, exploiting the human inclination to explore intriguing offers.

Quid pro quo attacks promise something valuable in exchange for information or access. Attackers contact victims under the guise of offering technical assistance, often through phone calls or emails, and request access to the victim's system. In return, the attacker provides a reward, such as software licenses or technical support. Unsuspecting victims willingly provide access, inadvertently giving attackers entry into their systems. Quid pro quo attacks play on the innate human desire for gain, demonstrating how the promise of something valuable can cloud judgment and lead to security compromises.

The consequences of successful social engineering attacks can be severe and far-reaching. From individuals to organizations, the fallout of falling victim to these attacks can extend beyond immediate financial losses. Identity theft resulting from phishing attacks can lead to a cascade of issues, including ruined credit scores and a prolonged recovery process. Spear phishing attacks targeting employees within organizations can lead to data breaches, financial losses, and damage to reputation. In the corporate world, successful social engineering attacks can compromise sensitive intellectual property, compromise critical infrastructure, and even lead to legal liabilities.

The pervasive and adaptive nature of social engineering attacks necessitates a multifaceted approach to mitigation. Technological solutions such as spam filters and multi-factor authentication provide valuable layers of defense, but the ultimate safeguard lies in the education and awareness of individuals. Comprehensive cybersecurity training empowers individuals to recognize red flags, exercise caution, and respond appropriately to suspicious requests. Organizations must foster a culture of cybersecurity awareness, ensuring that employees are equipped to identify potential threats and report them promptly. Providing individuals the information and skills to resist manipulation is the first step in the fight against social engineering attacks, which includes continual education efforts and simulated phishing exercises.

In conclusion, social engineering attacks highlight the intricate interplay between technology and human behavior in the digital age. As technology develops, so do the tactics employed by adversaries seeking to exploit human psychology. The evolution of social engineering— from generic phishing to highly personalized spear

phishing—underscores the adaptability and persistence of cyber criminals. The battleground is not just in the realm of technology but in the minds of individuals who must navigate a complex digital landscape. By cultivating cybersecurity awareness, fostering critical thinking, and embracing a proactive defense posture, individuals and organizations can fortify themselves against the allure of deception and emerge as formidable defenders of the digital realm. In the ongoing arms race between the art of manipulation and the power of education, the latter
stands as a beacon of hope in the fight against social engineering attacks.

User Awareness and Training

In the rapidly evolving landscape of cybersecurity, where technology intertwines with human behavior, the role of individuals as the first line of defense has never been more pivotal. The effectiveness of security measures depends on users' awareness and readiness as cyber threats become more focused and sophisticated. User awareness and training initiatives have emerged as a cornerstone of cybersecurity strategies, equipping individuals with the knowledge, skills, and mindset to recognize, respond to, and mitigate potential threats. This section delves into the critical realm of user awareness and training, exploring its significance, methodologies, impact on organizations and individuals, challenges, and the ever-expanding imperative of fostering a cyber-literate society.

User awareness constitutes the bedrock of cyber resilience, forming the foundation for secure digital environments. In an era where cyber threats extend beyond technical vulnerabilities to target the human element, educating users about potential risks is paramount. Cybercriminals exploit the inherent vulnerabilities of human psychology through techniques like social engineering, where deception and manipulation are the primary tools. Thus, cultivating user awareness is not merely a checklist item, but a dynamic and ongoing process that empowers individuals to identify and respond to threats proactively.

User awareness and training encompass a broad spectrum of topics beyond technical proficiency. While educating users about password hygiene, secure browsing, and safe email practices is crucial, cybersecurity training should encompass a deeper understanding of threat landscapes, the psychology of social engineering, and the role of individuals in maintaining organizational security. By fostering a holistic perspective that transcends technical jargon, individuals are better equipped to comprehend the nuances of cyber threats and make informed decisions.

Effective user awareness and training employ a multifaceted approach that engages and empowers users at various levels. Interactive workshops, seminars, and simulations provide hands-on experiences that mimic real-world scenarios. Simulated phishing exercises enable users to encounter and identify phishing attempts in a controlled environment, enhancing their ability to spot similar threats in the wild. Gamification leverages competitive elements to make training engaging and enjoyable, encouraging participation and knowledge retention. Additionally, continuous training campaigns that leverage microlearning modules, newsletters, and webinars foster a culture of ongoing cybersecurity awareness.

User awareness and training reverberate throughout organizations, transforming employees from potential liabilities into proactive defenders. Educated users serve as a formidable human firewall, identifying and thwarting threats before they can manifest into breaches. Reducing successful phishing attacks, data breaches, and security incidents can lead to substantial financial savings and safeguard the organization's reputation. Moreover, user awareness contributes to a culture of security, instilling a sense of responsibility among employees and creating a collective effort to protect digital assets.

Beyond organizational benefits, user awareness and training equip individuals with skills that transcend workplace settings. In an era where personal and professional lives are inextricably linked online, cyber threats have permeated all aspects of existence. The knowledge gained from cybersecurity training extends to personal online activities, allowing individuals to safeguard their digital identities, financial information, and online interactions. The empowerment of individuals to navigate the digital landscape with confidence and prudence contributes to a safer and more secure cyber ecosystem.

While user awareness and training offer immense promise, they also present challenges that demand careful consideration. Cybersecurity threats' transient nature necessitates frequent training content updates to reflect the evolving threat landscape. Additionally, balancing imparting technical knowledge and fostering a behavioral shift requires tailored approaches catering to diverse skill levels and learning styles. Ensuring sustained engagement and participation in training initiatives can be challenging in organizations with varying degrees of cybersecurity maturity.

As user awareness and training gain prominence, addressing the digital divide that can exacerbate disparities in cyber education is essential. Vulnerable populations without consistent technological or educational access may be disproportionately exposed to cyber threats. Initiatives aimed at bridging this gap, such as community workshops and public awareness campaigns, play a pivotal role in democratizing cybersecurity knowledge and extending its benefits to all segments of society.

In an era of digital transformation, the imperative to cultivate a cyber-literate society cannot be overstated. Governments, educational institutions, businesses, and individuals must collaborate to promote cyber education at all levels. Incorporating cybersecurity awareness into school curricula can instill foundational knowledge from an early age, fostering a generation that is inherently cautious and knowledgeable about online threats. Businesses must invest in continuous training programs that adapt to emerging threats, ensuring that employees remain vigilant and adept in the face of evolving challenges.

In conclusion, user awareness and training are a beacon of hope in the battle against an ever-expanding array of cyber threats. In a world where technology bridges geographical distances and connects disparate elements of life, protecting digital identities, financial assets, and personal information is paramount. Through comprehensive training, individuals are equipped with the tools to navigate the digital landscape with resilience and prudence, strengthening their security posture and contributing to a safer cyber ecosystem. As cyber threats continue to evolve, the power of knowledge remains an enduring and essential asset in the quest for digital security and the creation of a cyber-resilient society.

Insider Threats and Mitigation

In the intricate tapestry of cybersecurity, where external threats dominate headlines, a shadowy adversary often lurks within the confines of organizations: the insider threat. Insider threats emerge when individuals with privileged access, often employees or contractors, exploit their position to compromise data, sabotage systems, or steal sensitive information. Unlike external attackers, insiders possess intimate knowledge of an organization's infrastructure, making their actions potentially more damaging and harder to detect. To counter this hidden peril, organizations must adopt a comprehensive approach that combines technical solutions, robust policies, and a culture of vigilance to mitigate the risks posed by insider threats.

Insider threats are not confined to a single archetype; they span a spectrum of motives and behaviors. The threat landscape is multifaceted from the malicious insider seeking financial gain to the unwitting employee inadvertently compromising security. Insiders can be categorized as negligent (unintentionally causing harm), compromised (coerced or manipulated by external actors), and malicious (deliberately seeking to harm the organization). Each category demands a nuanced approach to detection and mitigation.

Identifying insider threats requires understanding the motives that drive such actions. Financial gain, revenge, ideological motivations, and a desire for personal recognition are common drivers. Monitoring for warning signs, such as sudden changes in behavior, unauthorized access attempts, or unexplained data transfers, can help organizations detect potential insider threats before they escalate.

Technical controls play a pivotal role in mitigating insider threats. Role-based access controls (RBAC) ensure that users have access only to the resources necessary for their roles, reducing the potential for unauthorized actions. User and entity behavior analytics (UEBA) tools monitor user activity, identifying anomalous patterns that may indicate insider threats. Data loss prevention (DLP) solutions can prevent unauthorized data transfers or access, adding an extra layer of protection against data breaches.

Comprehensive risk management strategies are essential in combating insider threats. Organizations should implement security policies that define acceptable use of company resources, specify consequences for policy violations, and outline clear reporting channels for suspicious activities. These policies should be communicated regularly and undergo periodic reviews to remain aligned with evolving threats.

A security-aware culture is pivotal in minimizing insider threats. Regular training programs can educate employees about the risks posed by insider threats, common attack vectors, and the importance of reporting suspicious activities. Organizations encourage a collective effort in threat mitigation by promoting an environment where individuals feel empowered to raise concerns without fear of retribution.

In the unfortunate event of an insider threat incident, a well-defined incident response plan is indispensable. Rapid detection, containment, and investigation are critical to minimize the potential damage. Monitoring activities should extend beyond prevention to encompass early detection and swift response, ensuring that incidents are addressed before they escalate.

Human resources departments are pivotal in insider threat mitigation. Effective communication between HR and IT/security teams can ensure that access permissions are promptly revoked when employees leave the organization. HR can also assist in identifying behavioral changes or issues that may raise red flags and require further investigation.

While implementing stringent controls to counter insider threats is essential, balancing trust and security is crucial. Overly restrictive measures can hinder productivity and create a negative work environment. A nuanced approach involves implementing the principle of least privilege, where access rights are limited to what is essential for each role, and closely monitoring high-risk areas without infringing on privacy.

The landscape of insider threats is ever-evolving, necessitating continuous improvement in mitigation strategies. Regular threat assessments, vulnerability assessments, and penetration testing help identify potential weak points in an organization's defenses. These assessments enable organizations to adapt their security measures in response to changing insider threat tactics.

Insider threat mitigation is not solely an IT concern; it requires collaboration across departments and levels. Open lines of communication between IT, HR, legal, and management are crucial for effective threat identification and response. Transparency about security policies and their rationale fosters an environment where employees understand their role in protecting the organization.

In conclusion, insider threats overshadow the cybersecurity landscape, representing a complex and often underestimated danger. As organizations embrace digital transformation, the potential for insiders to exploit their access magnifies. To address this menace, organizations must foster a culture of vigilance, establish robust technical controls, and implement comprehensive policies. By merging these efforts, organizations can unveil the hidden threats within and navigate the path to cybersecurity resilience, safeguarding their digital assets, intellectual property, and sensitive information from the shadowy specter of insider threats.

CHAPTER IV

Network Security

Firewalls and Intrusion Detection Systems

In the ever-expanding digital landscape, where data flows ceaselessly and cyber threats evolve at an alarming pace, the role of firewalls and intrusion detection systems (IDS) stands as a cornerstone in securing digital ecosystems. These technologies act as vigilant sentinels, guarding the digital perimeter against unauthorized access, malicious activities, and potential breaches. Firewalls serve as the first line of defense, while IDS operate as digital watchmen, alerting defenders to suspicious behaviors. Understanding the functions, types, and strategic deployment of firewalls and IDS is crucial in maintaining a robust cyber defense posture.

Firewalls are foundational network security elements, enforcing access controls between an internal network and the external world. Acting as gatekeepers, firewalls examine incoming and outgoing traffic based on predefined rules. Firewalls can be deployed at various points within a network, including at the network perimeter, within internal segments, and even on individual devices. They serve as the primary barrier against unauthorized access and potential cyber threats.

Firewalls come in several types, each tailored to specific security needs. Packet-filtering firewalls analyze incoming and outgoing data packets, allowing or blocking traffic based on predetermined criteria such as source IP, destination IP, and port numbers. Stateful inspection firewalls build upon packet filtering by tracking the state of active connections, allowing only authorized packets. Next-generation firewalls (NGFW) combine traditional firewall functionalities with deep packet inspection, intrusion prevention, and application awareness.

While firewalls control network traffic flow, IDS monitors and detects unauthorized or malicious activities. IDS operates in network-based (NIDS) and host-based (HIDS). NIDS analyzes network traffic in real-time, identifying patterns indicative of attacks or anomalies. HIDS, on the other hand, is deployed on individual devices to monitor for suspicious behavior at the host level. IDS are designed to raise alerts when predefined thresholds or patterns are met, signaling potential threats that require further investigation.

IDS employs two primary methods of detection: signature-based and anomaly-based. Signature-based detection involves comparing incoming data to known attack patterns or signatures database. When a match is found, an alert is triggered. Anomaly-based detection, on the other hand, establishes a baseline of normal behavior for a system and raises alarms when deviations from this baseline occur. This approach is particularly effective in identifying novel or zero-day attacks.

The most effective cybersecurity strategy leverages both firewalls and IDS in tandem. Firewalls build a barrier between trusted and untrusted networks, minimizing the attack surface. IDS complements this defense by providing real-time monitoring and alerts, enabling swift response to potential breaches. Together, these technologies create multilayered protection, reducing the likelihood of successful attacks and minimizing the impact of breaches.

Deploying firewalls and IDS comes with challenges. False positives—alerts triggered by benign activities—are common in IDS, potentially leading to alert fatigue. Tuning the systems to minimize false positives without compromising detection accuracy is a delicate balance. Additionally, as cyber threats become more sophisticated, attackers may employ evasion techniques to bypass these defenses. Regular updates, rule adjustments, and staying informed about emerging threats are essential in maintaining the effectiveness of firewalls and IDS.

The landscape of firewalls and IDS is continually evolving to meet the requirements of new technologies and threats. As organizations embrace cloud computing, mobile devices, and the Internet of Things (IoT), firewalls and IDS must adapt to protect these diverse and interconnected environments. Additionally, the rise of machine learning and artificial intelligence is shaping the development of advanced firewalls and IDS that can detect and respond to threats in real-time, making predictions based on behavioral analysis.

In conclusion, in the ceaseless symphony of digital interactions, firewalls and intrusion detection systems stand as the guardians of the digital realm. Their intricate dance of prevention and detection serves as a vital shield against the myriad of cyber threats that abound. Firewalls create barriers against unauthorized access, while IDS serve as vigilant watchers, sounding alarms when the harmony is disrupted. As organizations navigate the complex landscape of cybersecurity, the strategic deployment of firewalls and IDS remains essential to safeguarding data, preserving privacy, and ensuring the integrity of digital ecosystems.

Virtual Private Networks (VPNs)

In the expansive digital landscape, where data travels across borders and cyber threats lurk everywhere, Virtual Private Networks (VPNs) have emerged as vital tools for safeguarding privacy, securing communications, and circumventing online restrictions. A VPN creates an encrypted tunnel, shielding internet traffic from prying eyes and malicious actors. With the rise of remote work, data breaches, and concerns over online privacy, understanding the intricacies of VPNs is crucial for individuals and organizations seeking to navigate the digital wilderness with confidence and security.

A VPN is a technology that extends a private network across a public network, like the Internet. A VPN effectively shields online activities from surveillance and eavesdropping by encrypting data and routing it through servers in different geographic locations. This encrypted tunnel masks the user's IP address, making it hard for third parties to track online behavior, monitor communications, or trace the origin of data packets.

VPNs provide privacy and anonymity, allowing users to traverse the digital landscape without leaving a discernible trail of digital footprints. This is particularly crucial as governments, ISPs, and advertisers increasingly scrutinize and monetize users' online activities. VPNs obscure the user's true IP address, making it appear as if they are connecting from a different location. This enhances online anonymity and enables individuals to access region-restricted content and services.

Beyond privacy, VPNs bolster security by encrypting data in transit, safeguarding it from interception by hackers or cybercriminals. This is especially vital when using public

Wi-Fi networks, which are notorious hotspots for data interception. Encryption guarantees that even if data is intercepted, it remains indecipherable without the encryption keys.

VPNs come in various flavors, each tailored to specific use cases. Remote access VPNs enable individuals to securely connect to a private network from remote locations like home or a coffee shop. Site-to-site VPNs establish encrypted connections between multiple networks, often utilized by businesses to connect branch offices securely. Mobile VPNs offer protection for mobile devices, ensuring that data remains secure even while on the move. Beyond these, specialty VPNs cater to niche needs such as bypassing censorship, protecting against DDoS attacks, and maintaining anonymity.

Selecting a VPN provider requires careful consideration. The provider's logging policy, encryption protocols, server locations, and speed performance should be evaluated. A strict no-logs policy ensures that the VPN provider doesn't retain user activity data, enhancing privacy. Robust encryption protocols, such as OpenVPN and IKEv2/IPSec, are essential for robust security. The number of server locations affects connection speed and the ability to bypass geo-restrictions.

While VPNs offer numerous benefits, they are not a panacea. Users must be aware of potential limitations and risks. VPNs can introduce latency, affecting connection speed. Some websites and services may block or limit users' access through VPNs. Moreover, VPNs do not provide foolproof protection against all cyber threats; users must exercise caution, employ strong passwords, and update their devices.

A delicate balance exists between security and usability when using VPNs. While VPNs enhance security, they can also introduce complexities. Selecting servers, dealing with potential connectivity issues, and managing subscriptions can be overwhelming for some users. To strike a balance, choosing a VPN provider that offers user- friendly apps and interfaces is essential.

VPNs operate in a legal gray area in some jurisdictions. While VPNs are legal in many countries and serve as valuable tools for privacy, they can also be used for illicit activities. Users should be aware of the legal landscape in their region, as some governments have imposed restrictions or banned VPN usage. Transparent VPN providers openly disclose their legal obligations and practices.

In conclusion, as the digital frontier expands and cyber threats become more sophisticated, VPNs emerge as essential companions for the journey. They empower individuals and organizations to reclaim their online privacy, secure sensitive communications, and transcend geographical barriers. In a world where data breaches and surveillance are rampant, understanding the mechanisms, benefits, and limitations of VPNs empowers users to navigate the digital wilderness confidently, safeguarding their digital identities and data from the prying eyes of the digital realm.

Network Segmentation and Isolation

In the dynamic realm of cybersecurity, where threats multiply and evolve relentlessly, network segmentation and isolation have emerged as critical strategies to fortify digital defenses. These practices involve partitioning networks into smaller, distinct segments, creating virtual strongholds that confine potential breaches and limit the lateral movement of attackers. By erecting barriers within the digital landscape, organizations can minimize the impact of security incidents, contain potential breaches, and protect critical assets from compromise. Understanding network segmentation and isolation's principles, benefits, and challenges is pivotal in constructing resilient cyber architectures.

Network segmentation entails dividing a single network into smaller subnetworks, each with its own unique security policies and access controls. The aim is to categorize data flows and systems, minimizing the exposure of sensitive assets to potential threats. Segmentation can be implemented at various physical, virtual, and logical levels, tailoring the approach to an organization's specific requirements.

The benefits of network segmentation are multifaceted. First, it reduces the attack surface by restricting attackers' pathways. Even if a breach occurs, the attacker's lateral movement is constrained within the segmented environment, limiting the scope of potential damage. Second, segmentation enhances the efficiency of security measures. Resources can be allocated more effectively to protect critical assets, reducing the need for a one-size-fits-all approach to security. Lastly, compliance with regulatory requirements is facilitated as sensitive data can be isolated and protected within specific segments, ensuring data privacy and integrity. Network segmentation can be achieved through different strategies, each offering varying isolation.

Microsegmentation, for instance, involves segmenting at the individual workload level within a virtualized environment. This fine-grained approach provides granular control over communication flows but can also be complex to manage. Conversely, zoning divides a network into zones based on functional requirements, minimizing cross-zone traffic. Whatever the strategy, it's crucial to balance security and usability to avoid overly complex configurations that hinder operational efficiency.

While network segmentation creates distinct compartments, isolation takes defense a step further by physically or logically isolating critical assets from the broader network. Isolation ensures that sensitive systems and data are shielded from potential threats by removing them from the larger attack surface. This approach often safeguards high-value assets, such as financial systems, intellectual property repositories, and industrial control systems.

The advantages of isolation are compelling. Organizations reduce the risk of compromise and data breaches by isolating critical assets. Even if attackers breach the perimeter, their access to isolated assets remains limited. Moreover, isolation can simplify compliance efforts, as sensitive data can be maintained within a controlled environment. However, isolation can also introduce challenges. Managing isolated environments requires dedicated resources and oversight, and there's a risk of creating "security silos" that hinder collaboration and communication.

Implementing network segmentation and isolation demands careful planning and consideration. First and foremost, a thorough understanding of an organization's assets, data flows, and risk landscape is essential. Segmentation policies should be tailored to align with business requirements while prioritizing security. Managing complex segmentation configurations and isolation environments can pose challenges, requiring ongoing maintenance, updates, and coordination among various stakeholders.

Network segmentation and isolation are not standalone solutions but rather integral components of a holistic cybersecurity strategy. They complement other security measures, such as firewalls, intrusion detection systems, and access controls. Effective integration requires aligning segmentation policies with existing security policies, ensuring seamless coordination between technologies.

The network segmentation and isolation landscape continuously evolves to meet the demands of changing threats and technologies. As organizations embrace cloud computing, edge computing, and the Internet of Things (IoT), segmentation strategies must adapt to protect these diverse and interconnected environments. Additionally, software-defined networking (SDN) and Zero Trust architecture are reshaping network segmentation and isolation implementation and management.

Network segmentation and isolation emerge as formidable tools for constructing cyber strongholds in the intricate dance between digital connectivity and cybersecurity. These practices minimize the potential impact of security incidents and empower organizations to take proactive control over their digital landscapes. Organizations can erect barriers that impede attackers' progress and protect the crown jewels of their digital realm by compartmentalizing data, confining breaches, and isolating critical assets. Network segmentation and isolation remain steadfast strategies as the cyber landscape evolves, guarding against the ever-changing threats that lurk in the digital shadows.

CHAPTER V

Endpoint Security

Antivirus and Anti-malware Solutions

In the relentless cybersecurity battlefield, where malicious software spreads like a digital plague, antivirus and anti-malware solutions stand as stalwart sentinels, guarding against threats. These technologies, collectively known as endpoint protection, are the vanguards of defense against viruses, worms, Trojans, ransomware, and many other malicious software that seek to breach digital fortresses and compromise sensitive data. By employing sophisticated detection techniques and real- time monitoring, antivirus and anti-malware solutions play a crucial role in thwarting cyber threats, preserving data integrity, and maintaining the resilience of digital ecosystems.

Antivirus and anti-malware solutions are software programs designed to detect, prevent, and eliminate malicious software from computers and networks. These solutions act as a barrier against a wide range of threats, from traditional viruses that replicate and spread to more advanced forms of malware that employ encryption and obfuscation techniques to evade detection.

The effectiveness of antivirus and anti-malware solutions hinges on their detection capabilities. These solutions employ various techniques to identify malicious software. Signature-based detection involves comparing files and code against a database of known malware signatures. If a match is found, the software takes appropriate action. Heuristic analysis goes beyond signatures, identifying suspicious patterns of behavior that may specify the presence of new or unknown threats. Behavioral analysis monitors software behavior in real-time, flagging activities that deviate from typical usage patterns.

Modern antivirus and anti-malware solutions offer real-time protection, constantly monitoring system activities for signs of malicious behavior. They scan files as they are accessed, downloaded, or executed, instantly identifying and blocking threats before they can cause harm. Real-time protection is especially critical in the face of rapidly evolving threats that exploit vulnerabilities in software and hardware.

Antivirus and anti-malware solutions prevent infections and provide remediation when threats are detected. When malicious software is identified, these solutions attempt to remove or quarantine the threat, effectively neutralizing its impact. Some solutions offer additional features, such as system cleanup and recovery, restoring affected systems to their pre-infected state.

As cyber threats have grown in sophistication, antivirus and anti-malware solutions have evolved to meet the challenge. While effective against known threats, traditional signature-based approaches struggle to detect novel and zero-day attacks. To address this, modern solutions incorporate machine learning and artificial intelligence, enabling them to analyze vast amounts of data and identify previously unknown patterns of malicious behavior.

Despite their effectiveness, antivirus and anti-malware solutions face challenges and limitations. Attackers constantly innovate, employing evasion techniques that manipulate system vulnerabilities and evade detection mechanisms. Signature-based detection can be bypassed by modifying malware code or using encryption. Moreover, the sheer volume of new malware strains makes it impossible for signature databases to cover all threats.

Recognizing the limitations of traditional antivirus solutions, many cybersecurity providers offer comprehensive endpoint protection platforms. These platforms combine antivirus and anti-malware capabilities with firewall management, intrusion detection, and vulnerability assessment features. By integrating multiple security layers, these platforms provide a holistic defense against a broader spectrum of cyber threats.

Deploying antivirus and anti-malware solutions strategically is essential. Organizations should ensure that all endpoints, including workstations, servers, and mobile devices, are protected. Regular updates and patch management are crucial to ensure solutions can effectively counter emerging threats. Education and user awareness training also empower individuals to recognize and report potential threats, enhancing the overall security posture.

A key consideration in utilizing antivirus and anti-malware solutions is finding the right balance between performance and protection. While these solutions are vital for security, they can also impact system performance, especially on resource-constrained devices. Tuning the software settings and choosing solutions with minimal impact on system performance is crucial for a seamless user experience.

As the digital landscape develops, so will the threats that inhabit it. The future of endpoint protection lies in adaptive and proactive defenses. Behavior-based detection, predictive analytics, and real-time threat intelligence are trends that will shape the evolution of antivirus and anti-malware solutions. Integrating these technologies will enhance the ability to detect and respond to threats in real-time, safeguarding digital environments from the ever-changing threat landscape.

In the ever-evolving cybersecurity arena, antivirus and anti-malware solutions stand as the guardians of the digital realm. Their unyielding vigilance and advanced detection techniques are a powerful defense against the multifaceted threats that pervade the digital landscape. From traditional viruses to complex ransomware and advanced persistent threats, these solutions protect data, preserve privacy, and uphold the integrity of digital ecosystems. As organizations and individuals navigate the digital frontier, the partnership with antivirus and anti-malware solutions remains steadfast, ensuring that the digital realm remains fortified against the relentless onslaught of cyber adversaries.

Endpoint Detection and Response (EDR)

In the ever-evolving cybersecurity landscape, where threats loom large and breaches are a constant reality, Endpoint Detection and Response (EDR) has emerged as a pivotal strategy to fortify digital defenses. EDR represents a paradigm shift from traditional reactive approaches to a proactive, holistic defense posture. By monitoring and responding to endpoint activities in real- time, EDR empowers organizations to detect, investigate, and neutralize cyber threats at their earliest stages, to minimize damage and bolster cyber resilience. Understanding the principles, benefits, and implementation of EDR is crucial for navigating the complex terrain of modern cybersecurity.

EDR is a cybersecurity approach that focuses on monitoring, detecting, as well as responding to threats at the endpoint level. Endpoints, such as laptops, desktops, servers, and mobile devices, represent the frontlines in the battle against cyber threats. EDR solutions continuously collect and analyze endpoint data, enabling organizations to swiftly identify abnormal behaviors, potential breaches, and advanced threats that may bypass traditional security measures.

Central to EDR is real-time monitoring and threat detection. EDR solutions employ a combination of techniques, including behavior analysis, machine learning, and heuristics, to detect unusual or suspicious activities. By creating a baseline of normal behavior for each endpoint, EDR can quickly identify deviations that may indicate a potential threat. This proactive approach enables organizations to detect threats as they unfold, reducing attackers' dwell time within the network.

EDR detects threats and equips organizations with the tools to investigate and respond effectively. When an anomaly or potential threat is identified, EDR solutions provide detailed insights into the attack chain, including the origin of the threat, the techniques employed, and the scope of the breach. This information is invaluable for incident responders, enabling them to make informed decisions and implement targeted measures to contain and neutralize the threat.

The benefits of EDR are multifaceted. First and foremost, EDR shifts the focus from mere prevention to swift detection and response, reducing the time it takes to identify and neutralize threats. This is particularly crucial in an environment where attackers continuously innovate and adapt their tactics. Additionally, EDR provides organizations visibility into their entire endpoint ecosystem, facilitating proactive management, patching, and vulnerability mitigation. EDR also assists in meeting regulatory compliance requirements by providing audit trails and documentation of security incidents.

While EDR offers robust capabilities, it has challenges. EDR solutions require careful configuration and tuning to minimize false positives, ensuring that alerts are relevant and actionable. Additionally, EDR solutions generate large volumes of data, which must be effectively managed and analyzed to avoid overwhelming security teams. Moreover, EDR requires skilled personnel who can interpret and respond to alerts, underscoring the importance of cybersecurity expertise.

EDR is most effective when integrated with existing security measures. EDR solutions complement traditional antivirus and anti-malware software by providing a deeper level of visibility into endpoint activities. They also enhance security information and event management (SIEM) systems by providing real-time data on endpoint behavior, enriching the organization's overall threat detection and response capabilities.

Implementing EDR requires a strategic approach. Organizations must assess their risk landscape, identify critical endpoints, and align EDR deployment with their security objectives. Careful consideration should be given to the choice of EDR solution, evaluating factors such as scalability, compatibility with the existing infrastructure, and ease of use. Ongoing training and skill development for security personnel are essential to ensure that EDR capabilities are maximized.

As the cyber threat landscape evolves, EDR must adapt to meet new challenges. Machine learning and artificial intelligence will be pivotal in enhancing EDR capabilities. Predictive analytics will enable organizations to anticipate and prevent threats before they materialize. Additionally, EDR will likely extend beyond traditional endpoints to encompass IoT devices, cloud workloads, and edge computing environments.

In the ever-shifting cybersecurity arena, where threats evolve at the speed of innovation, Endpoint Detection and Response (EDR) emerges as a beacon of proactive defense. EDR's ability to monitor, detect, investigate, and respond to threats in real-time empowers organizations to stay ahead of attackers, minimizing damage and maintaining business continuity. By elevating endpoint security from a reactive to a proactive stance, EDR heralds a new horizon in cybersecurity defense, equipping organizations with the tools and insights needed to navigate the intricate landscape of cyber threats. As organizations strive to fortify their cyber resilience, EDR stands as a crucial sentinel, guarding the digital realm against the relentless tide of adversaries.

Mobile Device Management (MDM)

In the age of digital mobility, where smartphones and tablets have become indispensable tools for both personal and professional endeavors, Mobile Device Management (MDM) has emerged as a critical strategy for maintaining security, managing devices, and safeguarding sensitive data. MDM offers organizations a comprehensive framework to control, monitor, and protect mobile devices, ensuring that these devices remain productive assets rather than security liabilities. By centralizing management, enforcing policies, and implementing security measures, MDM navigates the complexities of the mobile landscape and empowers organizations to embrace the benefits of mobility while minimizing associated risks.

MDM is a solution-driven approach that enables organizations to manage and secure mobile devices across their networks. It encompasses a range of activities, from device provisioning and configuration to enforcing security policies and ensuring compliance. MDM aims to provide IT administrators with the tools and capabilities necessary to maintain a consistent level of security and functionality across a diverse array of mobile devices.

The proliferation of mobile devices in personal and professional contexts has brought about unprecedented challenges for organizations. The sheer diversity of devices, operating systems, and applications introduces complexities in maintaining consistent security measures. Furthermore, the potential for data breaches and the loss of sensitive information via mobile devices underscores the urgency of implementing effective MDM strategies.

MDM offers a plethora of benefits, chief among them being enhanced security. MDM significantly reduces the risk of data breaches by enforcing security policies, configuring devices to adhere to best practices, and remotely wiping data in the event of device loss or theft. Moreover, MDM enables organizations to streamline device deployment, automate updates, and ensure regulatory compliance, ultimately boosting operational efficiency.

Centralized management is at the core of MDM. This entails having a single point of control through which IT administrators can manage all aspects of mobile devices.

From provisioning new devices to monitoring their usage, enforcing security policies, and remotely troubleshooting issues, centralized management ensures consistent and efficient administration across the mobile landscape.

MDM allows organizations to implement and enforce security policies aligning with risk tolerance and compliance requirements. These policies can encompass a range of measures, including password policies, encryption, remote lock and wipe capabilities, and restrictions on app installations. Through MDM, organizations can ensure that devices adhere to these policies, regardless of their physical location.

Proper device configuration and provisioning are critical for security and performance. MDM streamlines the process of configuring devices to meet organizational requirements, ensuring that devices are set up with the necessary applications, email settings, security profiles, and network configurations. This reduces the potential for misconfigurations that could compromise security or impede productivity.

MDM also extends to application management and distribution. Organizations can use MDM platforms to manage app deployment centrally, monitor app usage, and block or allow specific apps based on security considerations. This capability is particularly valuable in preventing the installation of malicious or unauthorized applications that could compromise device security.

Bring Your Own Device (BYOD) trend is where employees use personal devices for work, poses unique challenges and opportunities. MDM solutions cater to BYOD scenarios by allowing organizations to partition work and personal data, ensuring that business information remains protected even on personal devices. Additionally, MDM enables organizations to implement containerization, segregating work and personal data within the same device.

While MDM is crucial for maintaining security, organizations must balance security with user privacy. It's essential to communicate the scope of MDM policies to users, ensuring transparency about the data being collected, monitored, and managed. Balancing security and privacy is pivotal to building trust among employees and users.

While MDM offers substantial benefits, it's not without challenges. Ensuring seamless integration with various mobile operating systems and device types can be complex. Additionally, managing user adoption and resistance to MDM policies requires effective communication and education. Moreover, the evolving landscape of mobile threats demands that MDM solutions remain flexible and adaptive to emerging risks.

As the mobile landscape continues to evolve, so too will MDM solutions. The emergence of the Internet of Things (IoT) and the integration of mobile devices into broader ecosystems will drive the need for enhanced MDM capabilities. Mobile Threat Defense (MTD), a subset of MDM, is evolving to address advanced mobile threats, while Unified Endpoint Management (UEM) aims to bring together MDM with traditional endpoint management under a single umbrella.

In the mobile era, where devices have become an extension of individuals and organizations, Mobile Device Management (MDM) emerges as a linchpin for security, manageability, and efficiency. By centralizing management, enforcing security policies, and configuring devices to adhere to best practices, MDM empowers organizations to navigate the complexities of the mobile landscape while safeguarding sensitive data. In a world where the boundaries between work and personal use blur, and the threat landscape evolves, MDM serves as a beacon of control, ensuring that mobile devices remain productive tools rather than security liabilities. As organizations embrace mobility as a strategic advantage, the partnership with MDM is pivotal, enabling them to harness the power of mobile technology while fortifying their cyber defenses.

CHAPTER VI

Data Protection and Encryption

Importance of Data Encryption

In today's interconnected and data-driven world, where sensitive information flows through digital pipelines and cyber threats lurk at every corner, data encryption stands as a formidable shield against potential breaches and unauthorized access. Encryption, the process of converting plain data into unintelligible code that can only be deciphered by authorized parties, plays a pivotal role in preserving sensitive information's confidentiality, integrity, and authenticity. From financial transactions and personal communications to critical business data, the importance of data encryption transcends industries and sectors, shaping the modern landscape of cybersecurity and underpinning digital trust.

Data encryption involves transforming plaintext data into ciphertext, making it incomprehensible to anyone without the appropriate decryption key. This cryptographic technique ensures that even if unauthorized individuals intercept the data, they cannot glean any meaningful insights from it. Encryption is a crucial component in the broader realm of information security, providing an extra layer of defense against cybercriminals, hackers, and malicious actors seeking to exploit vulnerabilities and compromise sensitive data.

Confidentiality lies at the heart of data encryption. By rendering data unreadable without the decryption key, encryption ensures that even if a breach occurs, the stolen data remains useless to unauthorized parties. This is particularly crucial in industries handling sensitive information, such as healthcare, finance, and legal services. Encryption guarantees that personal, financial, and medical data remains private and secure, preserving individuals' rights to privacy and safeguarding against identity theft, fraud, and unauthorized surveillance.

Encryption is a powerful defense mechanism in an era characterized by increasingly sophisticated cyber attacks and data breaches. Breached data is often rendered useless to attackers without the decryption key, minimizing the potential impact of a breach. Encrypted data acts as a last line of defense, ensuring that sensitive information remains protected even if other security measures fail. This is particularly important as cyber threats evolve, employing novel techniques to exploit vulnerabilities.

Encryption protects data from unauthorized access and maintains its integrity and authenticity. Using digital signatures and certificates in encryption ensures that data remains unaltered during transit or storage. This prevents attackers from tampering with the data and assures recipients that the data they receive is genuine and untampered. Encryption upholds the integrity of digital communications and transactions in a world where trust is paramount.

Many industries are subject to strict regulatory frameworks that mandate the protection of sensitive data. Encryption is often a requirement to meet compliance standards. For instance, in healthcare, the Health Insurance Portability and Accountability Act (HIPAA) and in the European Union, the General Data Protection Regulation (GDPR), emphasize data protection and often require the encryption of sensitive data. Organizations that fail to implement adequate encryption measures may face legal consequences and reputational damage.

Encryption can be applied at various data lifecycle stages: at rest and in transit. Encryption at rest guarantees that data stored on devices, servers, or databases remains protected even if physical hardware is compromised. Encryption in transit secures data as it traverses networks and communication channels. Both forms of encryption work in tandem to create a comprehensive security posture, protecting data wherever it resides or travels.

Effective encryption relies on robust key management. Encryption keys are the digital counterparts of physical keys, granting access to encrypted data. Managing encryption keys securely ensures that authorized users can decrypt the data while keeping unauthorized individuals at bay. Key management encompasses key generation, storage, distribution, rotation, and disposal. Poor key management practices can undermine the very security that encryption aims to provide.

While encryption is a powerful security tool, it must also be user-friendly to be effective. Complex encryption processes can deter users from implementing security measures. As a result, encryption solutions are evolving to become more intuitive and seamless, reducing friction while ensuring that data remains protected. This balance between security and usability is essential for widespread adoption and compliance with encryption practices.

As technology evolves, so too does the landscape of encryption. Quantum computing, for instance, can potentially disrupt traditional encryption methods by rendering current encryption algorithms vulnerable. In response, post-quantum cryptography is being researched and developed to withstand the computational power of quantum computers. This highlights the dynamic nature of encryption, as researchers and developers continuously innovate to stay ahead of emerging threats.

In the confusing realm of digital connectivity, where data fuels innovation and information is the lifeblood of modern societies, the importance of data encryption cannot be overstated. Encryption stands as a guardian of digital trust, preserving privacy, thwarting cyber threats, and upholding the integrity of information. It empowers individuals, organizations, and governments to embrace the benefits of the digital era without compromising security. As the digital landscape continues to evolve, encryption remains a steadfast ally, navigating the delicate balance between openness and security, ensuring that the digital vaults of today's world remain impenetrable to those who seek unauthorized access.

Encryption Algorithms and Methods

In the intricate cybersecurity landscape, where digital data flows ceaselessly and cyber threats persistently evolve, encryption algorithms and methods stand as the bedrock of safeguarding sensitive information. Encryption, the process of transforming plaintext data into unreadable ciphertext, ensures that data remains confidential and secure, even if intercepted by unauthorized entities. As the backbone of modern information security, encryption algorithms employ intricate mathematical techniques and principles to fortify digital communication, protect privacy, and deter malicious actors. Understanding the diverse array of encryption algorithms and methods is essential for navigating the complex realm of cybersecurity and preserving the sanctity of data in the digital age.

Encryption algorithms are the mathematical formulas that underpin the encryption process. They define how plaintext data is transformed into ciphertext and, conversely, how ciphertext is decrypted back into its original form. Encryption algorithms rely on keys, which are cryptographic strings that determine the transformation process. Two main categories of encryption algorithms exist: symmetric and asymmetric.

Symmetric or private-key encryption employs a single key for encryption and decryption. The sender and the recipient must share this key in advance to ensure secure communication. The simplicity and speed of symmetric encryption make it suitable for large volumes of data, such as data transmission or storage. Popular symmetric encryption algorithms include Advanced Encryption Standard (or AES), Data Encryption Standard (or DES), and Triple DES (or 3DES). AES, in particular, is widely adopted due to its strong security properties and efficiency.

A pair of keys—a public key to encrypt and a private key to decrypt—are used in asymmetric encryption, also known as public-key encryption. This eliminates the need for key exchange between sender and recipient. Messages encrypted with a recipient's public key can only be decrypted using their corresponding private key, ensuring confidentiality. Likewise, a digital signature generated with a sender's private key can be verified with their public key, guaranteeing authenticity. Notable asymmetric encryption algorithms include RSA, Diffie-Hellman, and Elliptic Curve Cryptography (ECC).

Hybrid encryption combines the strengths of symmetric and asymmetric encryption. It involves using symmetric encryption to encrypt the actual data and asymmetric encryption to encrypt the symmetric key. This approach capitalizes on the efficiency of symmetric encryption for bulk data while leveraging the security benefits of asymmetric encryption for key exchange. Hybrid encryption strikes a balance between speed, security, and manageability.

Encryption methods, known as modes of operation, determine how encryption algorithms are used to secure data in various scenarios. These methods dictate how data blocks are divided, combined, and encrypted. Common modes of operation include Electronic Codebook (ECB), Cipher Block Chaining (CBC), Counter (CTR), and Galois/Counter Mode (GCM). Each mode has unique properties for specific use cases, such as confidentiality, authentication, or streaming data.

In encryption, randomness plays a crucial role in enhancing security. Salting and Initialization Vectors (IVs) are mechanisms used to introduce randomness into encryption processes. Salting involves adding a random value to data before encryption, ensuring that identical plaintext produces different ciphertexts. Conversely, IVs are unique values used in encryption modes like CBC to prevent patterns from emerging in encrypted data. These techniques bolster encryption against rainbow table attacks and ensure the uniqueness of encrypted data.

The strength of encryption relies heavily on the length of encryption keys. Longer keys provide greater security, as brute-force attacks become more computationally intensive. For instance, AES supports key lengths of 128, 192, and 256 bits, with longer keys offering higher levels of security. However, longer keys also introduce performance overhead, necessitating a balance between safety and operational efficiency.

As the quantum computing field advances, traditional encryption algorithms' security landscape faces potential disruption. Quantum computers can solve specific mathematical problems used in encryption algorithms more efficiently, rendering some algorithms susceptible to attacks. Post-quantum cryptography is being developed to counter this threat, aiming to create encryption methods that remain secure even in the face of quantum computers.

Selecting the appropriate encryption algorithm and method depends on several factors, including security requirements, operational needs, and the threat landscape. Symmetric encryption is favored for its efficiency, while asymmetric encryption addresses key exchange challenges. Hybrid encryption combines these strengths. Encryption methods must align with use cases, whether it's securing stored data, transmitting information, or ensuring authenticity through digital signatures.

While encryption is paramount for security, it must also be user-friendly to ensure adoption. Complex encryption processes can deter users from employing security measures. User-friendly encryption solutions, such as secure messaging apps and email services, abstract the technical complexities, making encryption accessible to a broader audience without compromising security.

In the digital realm, where information traverses vast networks and cyber threats are omnipresent, encryption algorithms and methods stand as the silent sentinels guarding the gates of digital trust. Their mathematical intricacies and cryptographic principles form the backbone of modern cybersecurity, ensuring that sensitive data remains shielded from prying eyes and malicious intent. Encryption's importance transcends industries and sectors from securing financial transactions to protecting personal communications and underpinning critical infrastructure. As the cyber landscape continues to evolve, encryption remains a steadfast companion, upholding the principles of confidentiality, integrity, and authenticity in a world where data's sanctity is paramount.

Data Loss Prevention (DLP)

In the digital age, where vast volumes of data are generated, shared, and stored, the specter of data breaches and leaks looms large. Data Loss Prevention (DLP) emerges as a strategic bulwark against these threats, enabling organizations to monitor, detect, and mitigate the unauthorized movement or exposure of sensitive information. DLP is a multifaceted approach combining technology, policies, and employee awareness to fortify data security. By understanding the nuances of DLP, its methodologies, benefits, and challenges, organizations can proactively navigate the treacherous waters of data protection and safeguard their digital troves from the relentless tide of cyber threats.

DLP encompasses a set of strategies, tools, and practices designed to hinder the unauthorized disclosure of sensitive data. This may include proprietary information, personal identifiable information (PII), financial data, and intellectual property. DLP solutions monitor data at rest, in transit, and in use, ensuring that information is accessed, shared, and stored according to organizational policies and regulatory requirements.

DLP employs various methodologies to prevent data loss across multiple vectors. Content discovery involves identifying sensitive data through keyword matching, regular expressions, and document fingerprinting. Contextual analysis assesses the context in which data is used, ensuring access and sharing align with legitimate use cases. User and entity behavior analytics (UEBA) track user activities to identify abnormal behaviors indicative of data exfiltration. Network-based DLP monitors data flows across the network, flagging suspicious patterns or unauthorized transfers.

The benefits of DLP are extensive. Primarily, DLP safeguards data from leaks, breaches, and unauthorized sharing, reducing the risk of reputational damage, legal liabilities, and regulatory non-compliance. DLP also supports compliance with data protection regulations, such as GDPR and HIPAA, by ensuring that sensitive information is managed and protected under legal mandates. Moreover, DLP enhances operational efficiency by streamlining data management processes and reducing the burden of incident response.

DLP has challenges. False positives, where legitimate actions are flagged as violations, can hinder user productivity and undermine confidence in the system. Fine-tuning DLP policies and rules is essential to balance security and usability. Additionally, the diversity of data formats, the proliferation of endpoints, and the complexity of cloud environments pose challenges for DLP implementation. Ensuring seamless integration with existing security measures and user education about DLP policies is crucial for effective adoption.

DLP solutions can be categorized into two main types: endpoint DLP and network DLP. Endpoint DLP focuses on data protection at the source, on the devices where data is created and accessed. This approach effectively controls data movement on individual devices, preventing data leaks through removable storage, email, or cloud services. Network DLP, on the other hand, monitors data flows across the network, identifying and blocking unauthorized transfers. This is particularly important for securing data in transit and preventing data exfiltration.

A cornerstone of DLP implementation is data classification and labeling. By categorizing data based on sensitivity, organizations can tailor DLP policies to different types of information. Classification also aids in prioritizing incident response and ensuring that the most sensitive data receives the highest level of protection. Automated data labeling can streamline this process, enabling users to apply labels to documents and emails based on predefined policies.

Effective DLP implementation requires user awareness and training. Employees must understand the significance of data protection, the risks of data leakage, and the impact of their actions on organizational security. Regular training sessions can educate employees about DLP policies, teach them how to recognize and handle sensitive data, and encourage a security-conscious culture. Employees should also be empowered to report potential incidents and violations promptly.

The cloud services and remote work proliferation has transformed the data landscape, necessitating DLP solutions that extend to cloud environments. Cloud DLP monitors and protects data stored in cloud applications, ensuring that data remains secure even when accessed from various locations and devices. Integration with cloud services and APIs enables organizations to enforce DLP policies consistently across on-premises and cloud environments.

The modern data landscape presents unique challenges for DLP. The rise of shadow IT, where employees use unauthorized apps and services, can circumvent DLP controls. Encrypted traffic poses difficulties for network DLP, as inspecting the contents of encrypted data is challenging. Additionally, the increasing use of personal devices for work purposes in the era of BYOD requires adapting DLP strategies to secure data on diverse endpoints.

In a world where data is the lifeblood of organizations and the fuel for innovation, Data Loss Prevention (DLP) emerges as a sentinel guarding digital integrity. Through its multi-pronged approach, DLP mitigates the risks of data breaches, leaks, and unauthorized access, fortifying organizations against the ever-evolving landscape of cyber threats. By harmonizing technology, policies, and user awareness, DLP empowers organizations to harness the power of data while preserving its sanctity. As the digital frontier continues to expand, and threats persist in their ingenuity, the partnership with DLP is pivotal, ensuring that sensitive information remains shielded, confidentiality is upheld, and digital trust is sustained.

CHAPTER VII

Cloud Security

Cloud Computing Basics

In the digital age, where information is the currency of progress, cloud computing has emerged as a transformative force, reshaping how individuals and organizations access, store, and utilize data and applications. Cloud computing transcends the traditional confines of hardware and software, ushering in a paradigm shift that empowers users to leverage computing resources on-demand without physical infrastructure constraints. Understanding the basics of cloud computing, its models, deployment options, benefits, and challenges, is essential for navigating this skyward shift and harnessing its potential to drive innovation, agility, and scalability.

The core of cloud computing is the Internet-based delivery of computing services. Servers, storage, databases, networking, software, analytics, as well as intelligence are just a few of the resources that are covered by these services. Users can access and utilize these resources on a pay-as-you-go basis rather than buying and maintaining physical hardware, transforming computing into a utility similar to electricity.

PaaS (also known as Platform as a Service), IaaS (also known as Infrastructure as a Service), and SaaS (also known as Software as a Service) are the three main service models offered by cloud computing. IaaS provides users with virtualized computing resources, including virtual machines, storage, and networking. By offering a platform and development environment where users may create, distribute, and manage applications, PaaS offers a higher level of abstraction. SaaS delivers fully functional software applications over the internet on a subscription basis.

Cloud computing deployment models delineate how cloud resources are accessed and shared. The primary deployment models are Public Cloud, Private Cloud, Hybrid Cloud, and Multi-Cloud. Third-party providers control and operate public cloud services, which are accessible to the general public. Private cloud resources can be hosted on-premises or by a third-party provider and are exclusive to a particular enterprise. The components of both public and private clouds are combined in a hybrid cloud, enabling data and applications to be shared between them. Multi-cloud involves using multiple cloud providers to leverage specialized services and avoid vendor lock-in.

Cloud computing offers a plethora of benefits that fuel its widespread adoption. Scalability allows resources to be scaled up or down according to demand. This enables organizations to avoid overprovisioning or underutilization of resources. The pay-as-you-go model eliminates the need for upfront investments in hardware and infrastructure, allowing organizations to pay only for the resources they use. Cloud computing also offers flexibility, agility, and accessibility. Resources can be rapidly deployed, facilitating quicker time-to-market for new products and services. Cloud services can also be accessed anywhere with an internet connection, promoting remote work and collaboration.

While cloud computing provides numerous advantages, it also presents challenges that must be addressed. Security and privacy are concerns as data is stored off-premises. Organizations must implement robust security measures and ensure compliance with regulations. Vendor lock-in can occur if an organization relies heavily on a single cloud provider. Latency and connectivity issues can arise due to dependence on internet connectivity. Data transfer and migration can be complex; cost management requires vigilant resource monitoring.

Cloud computing is a basis of digital transformation, enabling organizations to modernize their IT infrastructure and pivot toward agile, data-driven operations. Cloud-based technologies such as artificial intelligence (AI), machine learning (ML), and big data analytics facilitate innovation and drive business insights. Cloud also promotes the development of Internet of Things (IoT) applications by providing a scalable infrastructure to process and analyze the huge amounts of data created by IoT devices.

In conclusion, cloud computing has ushered in a new era of computing that transcends physical limitations, opening doors to unprecedented scalability, flexibility, and innovation. From individuals to enterprises, cloud computing empowers users to harness computing resources on-demand, transforming how we work, collaborate, and innovate. By understanding the fundamentals of cloud computing, organizations can make informed decisions about deploying resources, selecting service models, and navigating challenges. As technology evolves, cloud computing remains the horizon that guides us toward a future where computing is not just a tool but an enabler of boundless possibilities.

Shared Responsibility Model

In the dynamic realm of cloud computing, where digital landscapes transcend physical boundaries, the Shared Responsibility Model emerges as a foundational framework for safeguarding the integrity of data and applications. As organizations embrace the agility and the scalability of the cloud, it becomes imperative to comprehend the intricacies of this model that defines the division of security responsibilities of cloud service providers (CSPs) and their customers. The Shared Responsibility Model forms the cornerstone of a collaborative approach to security, dictating the roles each party plays in upholding the confidentiality, integrity, and availability of assets in the cloud.

At its core, the Shared Responsibility Model establishes a clear distinction between the security responsibilities of CSPs and customers. This demarcation is based on the type of cloud services being utilized, such as IaaS, PaaS, or SaaS. In the case of IaaS, the CSP is responsible for safeguarding the physical infrastructure, while customers are entrusted with securing the virtual machines, operating systems, applications, and data that reside on that infrastructure. As the abstraction increases through PaaS and SaaS, the distribution of responsibilities evolves, with CSPs taking on more accountability for lower-level components.

The implications of the Shared Responsibility Model are profound, shaping how organizations approach security in the cloud. CSPs are responsible for implementing robust security measures at the infrastructure level, including data centers, hardware, and networking. They ensure that their services are delivered securely, safeguarding against physical threats and ensuring compliance with industry standards. On the other hand, customers are tasked with configuring their applications securely, managing user access controls, and encrypting sensitive data. This bifurcation requires customers to understand their security responsibilities within the cloud environment comprehensively.

While the Shared Responsibility Model offers a clear framework for cloud security, it also poses challenges that demand attention. Ambiguities in the division of responsibilities can lead to gaps in security coverage. Organizations might erroneously assume that the CSP manages specific security measures, leaving vulnerabilities unaddressed. Conversely, overestimating the extent of customer responsibilities could result in inadequate security implementations. This underscores the critical importance of robust communication, transparency, and education between both parties to ensure a harmonious and secure cloud environment.

The benefits of the Shared Responsibility Model are multifaceted. Clarity in delineated responsibilities fosters a deeper understanding of security measures, eliminating confusion and potential oversights. This clarity, in turn, contributes to streamlined compliance efforts, allowing organizations to meet regulatory requirements more effectively. The model's adaptable nature enables organizations to tailor security measures to their unique needs, ensuring that their applications and data are protected according to their specific requirements. Collaboration lies at the heart of this model, as CSPs and customers work hand in hand to secure digital assets, pool resources, and collectively identify and address potential vulnerabilities.

Organizations must undertake several key initiatives to implement the Shared Responsibility Model effectively.

Education and awareness campaigns are paramount, ensuring that stakeholders across the organization understand their respective security responsibilities. Establishing robust policies and guidelines aligning with the model's divisions provides a foundation for consistent security implementation. Regular internal and external audits help evaluate the adherence to security responsibilities and identify areas for improvement. Continuous monitoring mechanisms should also be implemented to recognize and respond to any security incidents or anomalies promptly.

In conclusion, the Shared Responsibility Model is a sentinel in the ever-changing cloud security landscape. It embodies a collaborative approach that defines the roles and responsibilities of CSPs and customers in protecting digital assets. As organizations harness the power of the cloud to drive innovation, agility, and growth, this model ensures that security remains a shared priority. Through effective implementation, continuous communication, and a commitment to collaboration, the Shared Responsibility Model serves as a compass, guiding organizations toward a secure and resilient cloud future.

Cloud Security Best Practices

In the modern digital transformation era, cloud computing has emerged as a cornerstone of technological advancement, enabling organizations to scale, innovate, and optimize their operations with unprecedented agility. However, migrating critical data and applications to the cloud introduces a new security challenge that demands meticulous attention. Cloud security best practices are essential to navigate this dynamic landscape, ensuring that the risks posed by cyber threats do not overshadow the benefits of the cloud. This section delves into the intricate domain of cloud security, exploring its significance, foundational principles, real-world application, challenges, and the evolving strategies that empower organizations to harness the cloud while safeguarding their digital assets.

Cloud security embodies the collaboration between cloud service providers (CSPs) and their customers to protect data, applications, and systems in the cloud environment. This collaboration is defined by the shared responsibility model, which delineates the division of security responsibilities between the CSP and the customer. While CSPs are responsible for safeguarding the underlying cloud infrastructure, customers are accountable for securing their applications, data, identities, and access management within the cloud. This shared approach underscores the importance of a cohesive security strategy that spans both sides of the cloud equation.

Robust cloud security is grounded in a set of foundational principles that guide organizations in their pursuit of a secure cloud environment. Encryption serves as a fundamental pillar, encompassing data encryption at rest, in transit, and during processing. Access management and identity governance ensure that only authorized applications and users can access cloud resources. Multi-factor authentication adds an extra layer of defense by requiring multiple verification forms before granting access. Regular audits, monitoring, and incident response planning contribute to a proactive approach that can identify and mitigate potential threats promptly.

Data protection is at the heart of cloud security, as data constitutes the lifeblood of organizations. In the cloud, data protection encompasses strategies including encryption, data classification, and data loss prevention mechanisms. Encryption transforms data into unintelligible formats that can only be deciphered with the appropriate keys, safeguarding sensitive information from unauthorized access. Data classification classifies data based on its sensitivity, allowing organizations to allocate appropriate security controls to different data types. Data loss prevention technologies prevent the accidental or intentional leakage of sensitive information from the cloud.

Cloud applications are instrumental in driving business innovation and efficiency. However, securing these applications requires a comprehensive approach beyond traditional perimeter defenses. Secure development practices, such as integrating security into the software development life cycle (SDLC), help identify vulnerabilities early in development. Web application firewalls (WAFs) provide additional protection by inspecting incoming traffic for malicious activities. Regular application testing, such as vulnerability assessments and penetration testing, identifies and mitigates weaknesses before adversaries can exploit them.

In the cloud, identity is the new perimeter. Effective identity and access management (IAM) is pivotal to controlling who can access cloud resources and what actions they can perform. IAM solutions enable organizations to manage user identities, enforce access policies, and maintain a centralized view of permissions. Role-based access control (RBAC) assigns permissions based on job responsibilities, reducing the risk of over-privileged accounts. Single sign-on (SSO) streamlines user authentication by enabling users to access many applications with a single set of credentials. IAM systems enhance security while simplifying the user experience, striking a delicate balance between access and control.

Cloud network security is a multifaceted endeavor that demands meticulous attention to network architecture, segmentation, and threat detection. Virtual private clouds (VPCs) enable organizations to create isolated network environments, preventing unauthorized lateral movement. Network segmentation subdivides cloud resources into smaller, isolated segments, reducing the potential blast radius of a breach. IDS/IPS, Intrusion detection and prevention systems, monitor network traffic for anomalies and known attack patterns. Cloud-native firewalls add layer of defense, allowing organizations to filter incoming and outgoing traffic.

As organizations migrate sensitive data to the cloud, compliance with industry rules and data protection laws becomes paramount. Cloud security must align with regulatory requirements such as the General Data Protection Regulation, Health Insurance Portability and Accountability Act, as well as Payment Card Industry Data Security Standard (PCI DSS). Organizations must ensure that cloud service providers adhere to these regulations, often requiring contractual agreements outlining data protection measures, breach notification procedures, and compliance auditing.

While cloud computing offers unprecedented benefits, it is not immune to challenges that can undermine security efforts. Cloud complexity can lead to misconfigurations and security oversights that expose organizations to risks. A lack of visibility into the shared responsibility model can create confusion regarding security responsibilities. Cloud migration introduces the challenge of securing legacy applications that were not created or designed for the cloud environment. Additionally, cloud resources' dynamic and elastic nature requires equally agile and adaptable security measures.

The future of cloud security is shaped by emerging trends that reflect the ever-evolving threat landscape and technological advancements. Cloud-native security solutions leverage artificial intelligence and machine learning to detect anomalies and patterns indicative of cyber threats. Zero trust architecture, which assumes no inherent trust within or outside the network perimeter, is gaining traction as organizations seek to bolster security in an increasingly interconnected world. Integrating security into DevOps practices, known as DevSecOps, enhances collaboration between development and security teams, ensuring that security is a fundamental aspect of the software development life cycle.

In conclusion, cloud security best practices constitute a delicate balancing act between harnessing the benefits of cloud computing and mitigating the risks accompanying it. As organizations embrace the cloud for its scalability, flexibility, and innovation, a comprehensive security strategy is non-negotiable. Organizations can confidently navigate the cloud landscape by adhering to foundational principles, safeguarding data, fortifying applications, orchestrating identities, and embracing compliance. Cloud security is not a destination but a continuous journey that demands ongoing education, adaptation, and collaboration between cloud service providers and their customers. Through the vigilance and dedication of cloud security practitioners, the digital skyline can remain clear of threats, empowering organizations to soar to new heights in the digital transformation era.

CHAPTER VIII

Application Security

Common Application Vulnerabilities (SQL Injection, XSS, etc.)

In today's increasingly interconnected digital landscape, the security of applications has become a critical concern. As technology advances, so do the tactics and methods employed by malicious actors to exploit application vulnerabilities. SQL injection and also Cross-Site Scripting (XSS) are two of the most prevalent and damaging vulnerabilities. These vulnerabilities can have severe consequences, from unauthorized access to sensitive information to complete system compromise. Understanding these vulnerabilities and implementing robust security measures is paramount to safeguarding sensitive data and maintaining the integrity of applications.

SQL injection is a type of cyber attack that targets databases by manipulating an application's structured query language (SQL) queries. It occurs when an attacker injects malicious SQL code into an input field, tricking the application into executing unintended database operations. This can result to unauthorized access to the database, disclosure of sensitive information, or even data manipulation. For instance, a login form vulnerable to SQL injection could allow an attacker to bypass authentication and gain unrestricted access to the application. Preventive measures against SQL injection include input validation, using parameterized queries, and employing web application firewalls that can detect and block malicious SQL code.

Cross-Site Scripting (XSS) is another critical vulnerability that affects web applications. XSS attacks entail the injection of malicious scripts into web pages that other users then view. This allows attackers to execute scripts in the context of the victim's browser, potentially stealing sensitive data like cookies, session tokens, or personal information. There are three principal types of XSS attacks: stored (where malicious scripts are permanently stored on a server), reflected (where scripts are embedded in malicious links), and DOM-based (where scripts manipulate the Document Object Model of a webpage). To mitigate XSS vulnerabilities, developers can sanitize user input, implement proper output encoding, and employ security mechanisms like Content Security Policy (CSP) to restrict the execution of untrusted scripts.

Beyond SQL injection and XSS, other common application vulnerabilities are worth mentioning. Cross-Site Request Forgery (CSRF) is an attack where a user is tricked into performing unwanted activities on a web application in which they are authenticated. This occurs because the application fails to verify the request's source, allowing attackers to initiate actions on behalf of the victim without their consent. Implementing anti-CSRF tokens, which are unique tokens associated with each user session, can help prevent this type of attack.

Insecure Deserialization is a vulnerability that arises when an application improperly handles serialized data, often obtained from untrusted sources. Attackers can utilize this vulnerability to execute arbitrary code, potentially leading to remote code execution or denial of service attacks. Proper input validation and using trusted serialization libraries are essential to mitigate this risk.

Security Misconfigurations occur when an application or its components are not properly configured, leaving them susceptible to exploitation. This could include default credentials, unnecessary services running, or exposed sensitive information. Regular security audits and following industry best practices for configuration can significantly reduce the risk of such vulnerabilities.

Broken Authentication and Session Management vulnerabilities stem from weaknesses in how an application handles user authentication and maintains user sessions. Poorly implemented authentication mechanisms can lead to unauthorized access, while insufficient session management can result in session hijacking or fixation attacks. Using secure authentication methods, implementing session timeouts, and using secure session tokens are crucial in addressing these vulnerabilities.

In conclusion, application vulnerabilities like SQL injection, XSS, CSRF, insecure deserialization, security misconfigurations, and broken authentication pose significant threats to the cybersecurity landscape. Developers, security professionals, and organizations must prioritize understanding and addressing these vulnerabilities during the development and maintenance of applications. Regular security assessments, code reviews, and adopting security frameworks can go a long way in fortifying applications against these common threats. As technology develops, so do the tactics of malicious actors, making continuous vigilance and proactive security measures indispensable in safeguarding sensitive data and ensuring the integrity of applications in an increasingly interconnected world.

Secure Development Lifecycle (SDLC)

In the rapidly evolving digital landscape, where software applications play an integral role in various aspects of modern life, ensuring the security of these applications has become a paramount concern. The Secure Development Lifecycle (SDLC) emerges as a systematic approach to developing software that prioritizes security at every stage of the development process. By integrating security practices from inception to deployment, organizations can build applications that are inherently robust, resilient, and better equipped to withstand the evolving threats posed by cyber adversaries.

The SDLC begins with a comprehensive requirement analysis and design phase, where security considerations are woven into the fabric of the application's blueprint. Identifying potential security risks early on allows developers to design countermeasures that align with the application's functionality. Threat modeling, a technique used during this phase, helps identify potential vulnerabilities and prioritize security measures. A well-designed architecture with secure design patterns forms the foundation on which subsequent stages of development rest.

The implementation phase involves writing code based on the design specifications. Here, secure coding practices play a pivotal role. Developers must follow coding standards that mitigate common vulnerabilities like the SQL injection, cross-site scripting (XSS), and buffer overflows. Adopting security-focused coding guidelines and using approved libraries and frameworks can reduce the attack surface significantly. Regular code reviews ensure that security flaws are detected and rectified early, preventing them from snowballing into more significant issues later on.

Testing is a cornerstone of the SDLC, encompassing various methodologies to identify vulnerabilities and weaknesses within the application. Dynamic Application Security Testing (or DAST) and Static Application Security Testing (or SAST) are two essential techniques used during this phase. SAST involves analyzing the application's source code to identify vulnerabilities, while DAST simulates real-world attacks to uncover vulnerabilities from the outside. Additionally, penetration testing assesses the application's resilience against targeted attacks. By addressing vulnerabilities at this stage, developers can remediate issues before deployment, reducing the likelihood of exploitation.

Integrating security into the deployment pipeline ensures that security mechanisms remain intact as the application moves from development to production environments. Continuous Integration (or CI) and Continuous Deployment (or CD) practices are complemented by Continuous Security (CS), which involves automated security testing and validation throughout the deployment pipeline. This iterative process allows for rapid detection and mitigation of vulnerabilities that might arise during the application's lifecycle.

The post-deployment phase of the SDLC involves ongoing monitoring and maintenance to ensure the application's continued security and functionality. Implementing intrusion detection systems, log analysis, and security incident response plans are crucial for identifying and responding to emerging threats. Regular software updates, patches, and vulnerability assessments are essential to address newly discovered vulnerabilities and maintain the application's security posture over time.

The adoption of the SDLC offers a multitude of benefits. By embedding security throughout the development process, organizations reduce the danger of security incidents as well as data breaches, safeguarding sensitive information and maintaining user trust. Moreover, the SDLC encourages collaboration between development and security teams, fostering a holistic understanding of security requirements. However, challenges exist, such as integrating security into an already established development process and ensuring all team members possess the necessary security expertise.

In an era where the digital landscape is fraught with increasingly sophisticated cyber threats, the Secure Development Lifecycle (SDLC) emerges as a pivotal strategy to build secure, reliable, and resilient software applications. Organizations can proactively address vulnerabilities and safeguard sensitive information by ingraining security practices from the inception to the deployment and maintenance of applications. While implementing the SDLC may present challenges, the long-term benefits in terms of mitigating security risks, maintaining user trust, and minimizing the impact of potential breaches far outweigh these challenges. As the software development ecosystem continues to evolve, embracing the principles of the SDLC is not just a best practice but a necessity to navigate the complex terrain of cybersecurity.

Web Application Firewalls (WAFs)

In today's interconnected world, web applications have become integral to businesses, organizations, and individuals. However, along with the benefits they bring, web applications also attract a myriad of security threats. Web Application Firewalls (WAFs) have emerged as a crucial defense mechanism in the realm of cybersecurity, offering protection against a wide array of attacks targeting web applications. These sophisticated security solutions provide a proactive shield by analyzing and filtering incoming traffic to identify and mitigate potential threats. This section explores Web Application Firewalls' significance, mechanisms, deployment, benefits, and challenges.

Web applications are exposed to a multitude of attacks, including SQL injection, cross-site scripting (XSS), cross-site request forgery (CSRF), and more. WAFs play a pivotal role in cybersecurity by acting as a gatekeeper between the web application and the user, intercepting incoming requests and responses to detect and thwart malicious activities. Their significance lies in their ability to protect sensitive data, maintain business continuity, and preserve user trust by preventing unauthorized access, data breaches, and potential damage.

WAFs employ a range of mechanisms to identify and block malicious traffic. They analyze incoming requests and responses, comparing them against predefined security policies and rule sets. Signature-based detection involves recognizing patterns of known attacks and blocking corresponding traffic. Anomaly-based detection identifies abnormal behavior by establishing a baseline of legitimate traffic and flagging deviations. Moreover, modern WAFs utilize machine learning and artificial intelligence to adapt to emerging threats dynamically, enhancing their accuracy and effectiveness.

WAFs can be deployed in various ways to suit an organization's needs. They can be hardware-based appliances, software solutions, or cloud-based services. The choice of deployment depends on factors like scalability, ease of management, and the specific architecture of the web application. Cloud-based WAFs offer the advantage of elasticity and global coverage, making them suitable for businesses with a geographically dispersed user base. On the other hand, on-premises solutions provide more control over the configuration and data, appealing to organizations with stringent compliance requirements.

The benefits of integrating WAFs into a cybersecurity strategy are manifold. First and foremost, WAFs provide real-time protection against a wide range of threats without requiring modifications to the underlying application code. This means that even legacy applications can be safeguarded without extensive redevelopment. Additionally, WAFs offer a quicker response to emerging threats than traditional patching methods. They also contribute to regulatory compliance by helping organizations meet industry-specific security standards.

While WAFs are potent tools, they are not without challenges. False positives, where legitimate traffic is incorrectly flagged as malicious, can lead to disruptions in user experience. Conversely, false negatives, where malicious traffic goes undetected, pose serious security risks. Balancing robust protection with minimal impact on performance requires fine-tuning and continuous monitoring. Additionally, WAFs might not be able to fully protect against advanced and zero-day attacks, emphasizing the need for a multi-layered security approach.

Web Application Firewalls (WAFs) have emerged as indispensable guardians of web applications in the ever-evolving landscape of cyber threats. Their ability to analyze traffic in real-time, detect malicious activities, and thwart attacks before they reach the application is a critical component of modern cybersecurity. By safeguarding sensitive data, preserving user trust, and preventing potential disruptions, WAFs contribute to a resilient online presence for businesses and organizations. While challenges such as false positives, false negatives, and the dynamic nature of cyber threats persist, the benefits of implementing WAFs far outweigh the drawbacks. As organizations rely on web applications for critical functions, embracing WAFs as an integral part of the cybersecurity strategy is essential to ensuring a secure and resilient digital ecosystem.

CHAPTER IX

Incident Response and Recovery

Incident Response Plan (IRP) Development

In today's digital age's dynamic and interconnected landscape, the occurrence of cybersecurity incidents is not a matter of "if," but "when." As organizations rely more heavily on digital infrastructure, the potential impact of cyber threats on business continuity, data integrity, and customer trust cannot be underestimated. To effectively mitigate the damage caused by security breaches, organizations must adopt a proactive approach by developing robust Incident Response Plans (IRPs). These plans outline the systematic steps to be taken when a security incident occurs, ensuring a swift, organized, and well-coordinated response. This section delves into the critical components, development stages, challenges, and benefits of creating an effective IRP.

A comprehensive IRP encompasses several critical components forming a cohesive framework for managing incidents. First and foremost, the plan should define the roles as well as responsibilities of the incident response team members. This ensures that each member knows their responsibilities during an incident and can act swiftly. The plan should include clear communication protocols to ensure timely dissemination of information among stakeholders. Additionally, it should outline the steps for identifying, classifying, and prioritizing incidents based on their severity. Escalation procedures, incident containment strategies, recovery measures, and post-incident analysis are other vital components that contribute to a well-rounded IRP.

The development of an IRP is a structured process that involves multiple stages. The initial step requires risk assessment, where an organization identifies potential threats and vulnerabilities. This assessment informs the creation of an incident classification framework, which categorizes incidents based on their impact and severity. Subsequently, an incident response team is formed, comprising individuals with expertise in various technical, legal, public relations, and management domains. The team collaborates to create the IRP, incorporating the critical components mentioned earlier. After development, the plan is tested through tabletop exercises and simulations to identify gaps and refine procedures. Regular updates based on lessons learned and changes in the threat landscape ensure the plan's relevance over time.

Developing an effective IRP is not without challenges. One of the primary challenges is obtaining buy-in from stakeholders across the organization. Convincing leadership of the importance of investing time and resources in IRP development can take time and effort. Furthermore, the dynamic nature of cyber threats requires constant updates to the plan to address emerging risks adequately. Ensuring the plan remains current and aligned with industry best practices can be resource-intensive. Additionally, striking the right balance between swift response and thorough investigation can be challenging, as hasty actions might exacerbate the situation.

Despite the challenges, the benefits of a well-developed IRP are numerous. Foremost among these is the ability to minimize the impact of security incidents. A swift and organized response can mitigate data breaches, prevent data loss, and maintain business continuity. IRPs also enhance an organization's resilience by facilitating the identification and containment of incidents before they escalate. Moreover, a comprehensive IRP demonstrates the organization's commitment to cybersecurity and can foster trust among customers, partners, and stakeholders. The lessons learned from incident analysis can improve the organization's overall security posture, leading to fewer incidents in the future.

Organizations must prioritize their ability to respond effectively to incidents in a digital landscape fraught with ever-evolving cyber threats. Developing an Incident Response Plan (IRP) provides a structured framework for managing security breaches, protecting data, and maintaining business continuity. By defining roles, responsibilities, communication protocols, and incident handling procedures, an IRP ensures that the organization is prepared to respond swiftly and efficiently to security incidents. While challenges such as stakeholder buy-in and plan maintenance persist, the benefits of a well-developed IRP in terms of minimizing damage, enhancing resilience, and fostering trust far outweigh the drawbacks. As cyber threats evolve, the importance of a robust IRP cannot be overstated, making its development an essential factor of any organization's cybersecurity strategy.

Cybersecurity Incident Types and Categories

In the interconnected digital landscape of the modern world, the ever-expanding array of cyber threats poses a formidable challenge to individuals, organizations, and governments alike. Cybersecurity incidents encompass a broad spectrum of malicious activities that target digital assets, compromise data integrity, and disrupt normal operations. From data breaches and malware attacks to insider threats and denial-of-service (DoS) attacks, the categories of cybersecurity incidents are as diverse as they are disruptive. This section delves into the intricacies of cybersecurity incident types and categories, examining their characteristics, real-world examples, impacts, and the multidimensional strategies cybersecurity professionals employ to thwart and mitigate these threats.

Cybersecurity incidents refer to any unauthorized or malicious activities that compromise digital assets' confidentiality, integrity, or availability. The motives behind these incidents vary, ranging from financial gain and corporate espionage to ideological reasons and nation-state operations. As the digital landscape becomes more interconnected and complex, the types of incidents have multiplied, demanding continuous vigilance and innovative defenses.

Data breaches are one of the most pervasive and damaging forms of cybersecurity incidents. Attackers infiltrate systems to steal sensitive information, such as personal identifiable information (PII), credit card details, and healthcare records. The fallout from data breaches extends beyond financial losses to potential identity theft, legal liabilities, and reputational damage. Notable data breaches include the Equifax breach of 2017, where cybercriminals compromised the personal information of nearly 147 million individuals, underscoring the immense impact of such incidents.

Malware attacks encompass a range of malicious software that infiltrates systems to disrupt operations, steal information, or facilitate further attacks. Malware comes in various forms, like worms, viruses, Trojans, ransomware, and spyware. Ransomware attacks, such as the WannaCry attack of 2017, encrypt victims' data and demand ransom payments in exchange for decryption keys. The proliferation of malware attacks highlights the need for robust cybersecurity measures that span prevention, detection, and incident response.

Insider threats emerge from individuals within an organization who misuse their access privileges to compromise security. These threats can be malicious, arising from disgruntled employees or insiders with ulterior motives, or inadvertent, as in the case of employees who unknowingly expose sensitive information. Edward Snowden's leaked classified National Security Agency (NSA) documents in 2013 serves as a high-profile example of an insider threat, highlighting the complexities of securing organizations from those within their ranks.

Denial-of-Service (DoS) and Distributed Denial-of-Service (DDoS) Attacks seek to overwhelm systems, networks, or services, rendering them inaccessible to legitimate users. In a DoS attack, a single source inundates a target with traffic, causing it to become unreachable. DDoS attacks amplify the impact by orchestrating many compromised devices, forming a botnet that launches a coordinated assault. The 2016 Dyn attack, which disrupted internet services across the United States, exemplifies the widespread consequences of DDoS attacks.

Phishing attacks exploit human psychology to trick individuals into divulging sensitive or personal information, such as passwords or credit card details. These attacks often employ deceptive emails, messages, or websites that impersonate legitimate entities. Spear phishing is a targeted variant that tailors attacks to specific individuals or organizations, using personalized information to increase credibility. Social engineering attacks extend beyond phishing to include tactics like pretexting, baiting, and quid pro quo, all manipulating human behavior to gain access or information.

Advanced Persistent Threats (APTs) are stealthy, sophisticated attacks that target specific entities, often with the backing of nation-states or well-funded adversaries. These attacks involve a prolonged intrusion that aims to remain undetected while exfiltrating sensitive information. Stuxnet, discovered in 2010, exemplifies an APT, as it targeted Iranian nuclear facilities and disrupted industrial control systems. APTs challenge traditional incident response strategies, demanding advanced threat detection and intelligence-driven defense.

Ransomware attacks have gained prominence recently, leveraging encryption to keep victims' data hostage until a ransom is paid. The attack surface has expanded beyond individuals to include businesses, healthcare institutions, and even municipalities. The 2021 attack on Colonial Pipeline, which disrupted fuel supply across the East Coast of the United States, underscored the real-world consequences of ransomware attacks. The increasing prevalence of ransomware highlights the need for robust backup and recovery strategies and proactive cybersecurity measures.

Supply chain attacks target the software and hardware components that organizations rely on. Adversaries compromise trusted vendors and introduce malicious code or vulnerabilities into their products, compromising the integrity of the supply chain. The SolarWinds supply chain attack in 2020, which affected numerous organizations by targeting software updates, exemplifies the far-reaching impact of such attacks. These incidents underscore the importance of robust vendor risk management and continuous monitoring of supply chain components.

Critical infrastructure attacks target essential systems that underpin society, such as power grids, water treatment facilities, and transportation networks. These attacks can have catastrophic consequences, affecting digital operations and endangering human lives. The Stuxnet worm, discovered in 2010, targeted industrial control systems, highlighting the potential of cyber attacks to disrupt physical infrastructure. Protecting critical infrastructure demands a convergence of cybersecurity and physical security measures.

In conclusion, the breadth and depth of cybersecurity incident types underscore cyber threats' relentless and adaptive nature. As technology evolves, adversaries continue to exploit vulnerabilities for financial gain, espionage, disruption, and ideological reasons. Defending against this spectrum of threats requires a multifaceted approach encompassing prevention, detection, incident response, and collaboration among organizations and governments. By understanding the intricacies of cybersecurity incident types and categories, cybersecurity professionals stand ready to face the evolving landscape and safeguard the digital frontier from the ever-present and multifarious threats that seek to compromise it.

Post-Incident Analysis and Improvement

In the dynamic landscape of cybersecurity, where threats are ever-evolving and attacks are inevitable, organizations must adopt a proactive and holistic approach to safeguard their digital assets. While preventive measures are crucial in thwarting cyber threats, post-incident analysis and improvement are equally important aspects of a robust cybersecurity strategy. This process involves meticulously examining the aftermath of a security incident, understanding the root causes, and implementing corrective actions to enhance resilience and prevent future occurrences. This section delves into the significance of post-incident analysis, the key components of the process, the challenges, and how organizations can derive lasting benefits from this critical endeavor.

Post-incident analysis is a cornerstone of effective cybersecurity by transforming security incidents into valuable learning opportunities. Its primary purpose is to gain insights into the incident's origin, progression, and impact. While preventing incidents is vital, understanding how they occurred can provide profound insights into an organization's vulnerabilities, misconfigurations, and gaps in security practices. This understanding enables organizations to rectify immediate issues and build a more resilient defense against future threats. By examining the timeline of events, tactics used by attackers, and the effectiveness of response measures, organizations can tailor their strategies for improved incident detection, response, and mitigation.

Post-incident analysis is a multifaceted process that encompasses several key components. First, it involves a thorough investigation into the incident's scope and impact. This includes assessing compromised systems, identifying compromised data, and gauging the extent of unauthorized access. Understanding the attack vector is equally crucial, as it sheds light on the exploited vulnerability or misconfiguration. A deep dive into the incident's progression helps uncover how attackers moved laterally within the network, the tools they employed, and the data they targeted. This analysis is complemented by evaluating the organization's response, highlighting strengths and weaknesses. The ultimate goal is to identify improvement areas and develop strategies that enhance the organization's overall security posture.

Despite its undeniable benefits, post-incident analysis presents several challenges that organizations must navigate. One such challenge is the complex nature of modern cyber attacks, where attackers often employ sophisticated techniques to obfuscate their activities. Additionally, the scarcity of skilled cybersecurity professionals can hinder the depth and speed of the analysis process. The pressure to quickly restore operations after an incident can also lead organizations to bypass in-depth analysis in favor of rapid recovery. Furthermore, the fear of reputational damage may discourage organizations from sharing incident details, limiting the broader cybersecurity community's ability to learn and adapt.

The primary benefit of post-incident analysis is the knowledge gained from dissecting the incident's anatomy. This knowledge empowers organizations to bolster their cybersecurity practices, thereby preventing similar incidents in the future. A comprehensive analysis may reveal vulnerabilities that need immediate patching or misconfigurations that require rectification. Lessons learned can also inform adjustments to incident response plans, ensuring the organization is better equipped to handle similar situations. Furthermore, sharing incident details with the broader cybersecurity community fosters collaboration, collective learning, and the development of innovative countermeasures.

Post-incident analysis should be viewed as an iterative process rather than a one-time task. As threats evolve, organizations must continuously refine their strategies and measures. This involves maintaining an open and learning-oriented culture, where each incident is seen as an opportunity to adapt and improve. Regularly updating security policies, procedures, and technologies is essential to stay ahead of emerging threats. Collaborating with other firms, sharing threat intelligence, and engaging with cybersecurity experts contribute to a proactive and adaptive cybersecurity approach.

In the realm of cybersecurity, prevention and preparation go hand in hand. Post-incident analysis and improvement serve as the linchpin between these two crucial aspects. By dissecting the anatomy of incidents, understanding their origins, and implementing corrective measures, organizations can fortify their defenses, enhance their resilience, and ultimately reduce the impact of future threats. Challenges notwithstanding, the benefits of post-incident analysis in terms of learning, growth, and collaboration far outweigh the obstacles. As technology continues to advance and attackers become increasingly sophisticated, organizations that embrace post-incident analysis as a cornerstone of their cybersecurity strategy are better poised to navigate the ever-evolving cyber threat landscape with confidence and agility.

CHAPTER X

Future Trends in Cybersecurity

AI and Machine Learning in Cybersecurity

In cybersecurity, the perpetual battle between attackers and defenders has taken on a new dimension with the appearance of Machine Learning (ML) and Artificial Intelligence (AI). These transformative technologies have ushered in an era where intelligent automation is harnessed to fortify digital defenses, detect anomalies, and respond to threats quickly and accurately. This section delves into the profound impact of AI and ML on cybersecurity, exploring their applications, benefits, challenges, and the evolving landscape of intelligent cyber defense.

The marriage of AI and ML with cybersecurity has given rise to many applications that redefine the security landscape. One of the most prominent applications is threat detection. AI and ML algorithms can analyze massive volumes of data to identify subtle patterns indicative of malicious activity. Intrusion Detection Systems (or IDS) and Intrusion Prevention Systems (or IPS) leverage these technologies to discern anomalies in network traffic and flag potential threats in real-time. Additionally, AI-powered anomaly detection can identify deviations from normal user behavior, thus aiding in the early identification of insider threats.

Another critical application lies in the realm of malware detection and prevention. Traditional signature-based methods are often inadequate against rapidly evolving malware variants. AI-driven solutions can learn from the characteristics of known malware and discern common traits, allowing for the proactive detection of previously unseen threats. Moreover, AI-powered sandboxes can analyze suspicious files in a controlled environment to identify their behavior and potential impact, aiding in timely mitigation.

The integration of AI and ML offers a multitude of benefits in the realm of cybersecurity. One of the most significant advantages is processing and analyzing vast amounts of data at speeds that far exceed human capabilities. This allows real-time threat detection and response, which is critical in an era where cyberattacks occur at an unprecedented pace. Furthermore, AI and ML algorithms can adapt and learn from new data, allowing them to evolve alongside emerging threats without constant manual intervention.

AI-powered solutions also enhance accuracy. By leveraging machine learning models trained on large datasets, organizations can significantly reduce false positives and negatives in threat detection. This accuracy improves the efficiency of cybersecurity operations and reduces the burden on human analysts who can then focus on more complex tasks requiring human judgment.

While AI and ML offer tremendous potential, they are not without challenges. One significant challenge lies in the potential for adversarial attacks. Attackers can exploit the vulnerabilities of AI and ML models by manipulating inputs to evade detection. Ensuring the robustness of these models against such attacks requires ongoing research and development. Additionally, AI and ML models can generate false positives when exposed to novel, benign behavior, leading to unnecessary alerts.

Striking the right balance between accuracy and alert fatigue remains a challenge.

Integrating AI and ML in cybersecurity is an evolving field, with continuous innovations shaping its trajectory. As AI models become more sophisticated, they can assist in analyzing massive threat intelligence feeds, aiding in identifying emerging threats. AI-powered predictive analytics can enable organizations to forecast potential vulnerabilities and plan proactive mitigation measures. AI-driven orchestration and automation can streamline incident response processes, ensuring rapid and well-coordinated actions during security incidents.

The convergence of AI and ML with cybersecurity has ushered in a novel era of intelligent automation that is transforming how organizations defend against digital threats. From real-time threat detection to adaptive malware prevention, these technologies offer many applications that enhance accuracy, speed, and overall cybersecurity posture. However, the challenges posed by adversarial attacks and the need to balance accuracy and alert fatigue underscore the ongoing need for research, development, and collaboration within the field. As technology continues to develop, AI and ML will remain instrumental in the fight against cyber threats, empowering defenders with the tools needed to stay one step ahead in the ever-evolving environment of cybersecurity.

IoT Security Challenges

The Internet of Things (IoT) devices proliferation has ushered in an era of unparelleled connectivity and convenience. IoT has transformed how we interact with our surroundings, from smart homes to industrial automation. However, this wave of innovation comes with a significant caveat: the challenges it poses to cybersecurity. The interconnected nature of IoT devices and their integration into critical infrastructure presents a myriad of security vulnerabilities that attackers can exploit. This section delves into the intricate landscape of IoT security challenges, discussing the nature of the threats, the reasons behind their vulnerabilities, potential consequences, and strategies to enhance IoT security.

IoT devices encompass many interconnected objects, including sensors, actuators, vehicles, appliances, and more. These devices collect and exchange data over networks, enabling them to interact with each other and with humans. However, this very interconnectivity is at the heart of IoT security challenges. The vast number of diverse devices and their often resource-constrained nature make traditional security approaches inadequate. Moreover, the critical role many IoT devices play in controlling infrastructure and systems amplifies the potential impact of a breach.

Several factors contribute to the vulnerabilities inherent in IoT devices. Many IoT manufacturers prioritize functionality and time-to-market over security, leading to the deployment of devices with inadequate security measures. Firmware and software updates are crucial for patching vulnerabilities and are often overlooked or not implemented promptly. IoT devices are also prone to using default credentials, making them easy targets for attackers. Furthermore, the lack of industry-wide security standards for IoT devices hinders the establishment of uniform security practices.

IoT devices are susceptible to various security threats that compromise data, privacy, and physical safety. Botnets, where compromised devices are used to launch attacks, can wreak havoc on networks through Distributed Denial of Service (DDoS) attacks. Unauthorized access to IoT devices can lead to data breaches, exposing sensitive information. Tampering with IoT devices can manipulate their functionality, leading to physical damage or even loss of life in critical applications like healthcare or industrial control systems. Privacy breaches are also a concern, as IoT devices collect personal data that malicious actors can exploit.

The consequences of IoT breaches can be far-reaching and severe. In industrial settings, a breach in IoT devices controlling critical infrastructure can lead to operational disruptions, financial losses, and even environmental hazards. In the consumer realm, compromised IoT devices can compromise home security systems, expose personal information, and render smart appliances vulnerable to unauthorized control. The interconnected nature of IoT devices also means that a breach in one device can lead to a chain reaction of compromises across the network.

Enhancing IoT security requires a multifaceted approach that involves manufacturers, developers, users, and regulatory bodies. Manufacturers should prioritize security from the design phase, implement regular software updates, and adhere to industry security standards. Developers should follow secure coding practices and consider the entire IoT ecosystem when designing security measures. Users should change default passwords, update firmware, and segment their IoT devices from critical networks. Regulatory bodies can play a pivotal role by enforcing security standards and ensuring IoT devices meet specific security criteria before entering the market.

In conclusion, the transformative potential of IoT devices is undeniable, but their integration into our lives and critical systems comes with a responsibility to address the security challenges they bring. The interconnected nature of IoT devices and their diverse landscape make securing them a complex endeavor. As the Internet of Things expands, mitigating IoT security vulnerabilities becomes paramount. A collaborative effort among manufacturers, developers, users, and regulatory bodies is crucial to establish a secure foundation for IoT devices. Only
through these combined efforts can we harness the benefits of IoT while safeguarding against the potential risks it poses to our digital lives and the broader societal landscape.

Quantum Computing's Implications for Cybersecurity

The evolution of quantum computing represents a revolutionary leap in computational power, promising to reshape industries, accelerate scientific research, and solve complex problems that were once deemed intractable. However, this quantum leap also introduces profound implications for cybersecurity, potentially rendering existing cryptographic techniques obsolete and demanding a reevaluation of security paradigms. Quantum computing's ability to solve problems exponentially faster than classical computers poses both opportunities and challenges for the realm of cybersecurity. This section delves into the intricate landscape of quantum computing's implications for cybersecurity, exploring its foundational principles, cryptographic impact, quantum-resistant strategies, global ramifications, and the ongoing quest to safeguard the digital future.

Quantum computing make use of the principles of quantum mechanics to perform calculations in ways that classical computers cannot. Classical computers rely on bits in states of 0 or 1, while quantum computers use quantum bits, or qubits, that can exist simultaneously in multiple states due to superposition. This property enables quantum computers to solve particular problems exponentially faster than classical computers, with potential applications ranging from drug discovery and optimization to simulating quantum systems.

One of the most major implications of quantum computing for cybersecurity lies in its potential to break commonly used cryptographic algorithms. Many encryption methods, including RSA and ECC (Elliptic Curve Cryptography), depend on the difficulty of factoring large numbers. Quantum computers can exploit Shor's algorithm to factor large numbers exponentially faster than classical computers, rendering these encryption methods vulnerable. As a result, the security of digital communication, data storage, and online transactions could be compromised if quantum computers reach a sufficient level of maturity.

Researchers are developing quantum-resistant cryptographic techniques to address the threat posed by quantum computing. These cryptographic methods are designed to remain secure even in the face of attacks from quantum computers. Lattice-based cryptography, code-based cryptography, and multivariate polynomial cryptography are examples of quantum-resistant techniques that base their security on problems that quantum computers have not demonstrated an advantage in solving. As quantum computing's development progresses, adopting these techniques becomes crucial to maintaining the confidentiality and integrity of digital communication.

The transition from classical to quantum-resistant cryptography poses unique challenges. Organizations must prepare for a heterogeneous environment where classical and quantum-resistant cryptography coexist. The National Institute of Standards and Technology (also known as NIST) has led efforts to standardize post-quantum cryptographic algorithms through a public competition, reflecting the collaborative global effort to address quantum computing's implications for cybersecurity. Adopting standardized post-quantum algorithms will mark a critical step in securing digital communication in the quantum age.

While quantum computing poses challenges, quantum mechanics also offers potential solutions through quantum key distribution (QKD). QKD leverages the principles of quantum mechanics to establish secure cryptographic keys between parties. The fundamental properties of quantum mechanics ensure that any attempt to intercept or eavesdrop on the key exchange would be detectable, providing a high level of security. While QKD has theoretical promise, practical challenges and limitations, such as distance constraints and the need for specialized hardware, must be overcome for widespread adoption.

The implications of quantum computing for cybersecurity extend beyond technical challenges to geopolitical considerations. Nation-states and actors with access to advanced quantum computers could break encrypted communications, gaining an advantage in intelligence and cyber operations. This raises questions about the balance between security and technological advancement. International collaboration and norms will be essential to ensure that quantum capabilities are used responsibly and do not undermine the privacy and security of individuals, organizations, and nations.

As quantum computing's development progresses, the cybersecurity landscape is marked by uncertainty and the ongoing pursuit of quantum-safe security. Organizations must assess their digital assets, communication channels, and data protection strategies to determine their vulnerability to quantum threats. Investments in quantum-resistant cryptography, post-quantum algorithms, and secure key management systems are pivotal to maintaining the integrity of digital ecosystems. The cooperation of governments, industries, and academia is imperative in ensuring that the transition to quantum-safe security is seamless and effective.

In conclusion, quantum computing's implications for cybersecurity demand a proactive and collaborative response. The paradigm shift introduced by quantum computing necessitates reevaluating cryptographic strategies, a commitment to quantum-resistant solutions, and a global dialogue about the responsible use of quantum capabilities. As quantum computers advance and the threat landscape evolves, organizations must stay informed about the latest developments, invest in research and development, and engage in partnerships to fortify their digital defenses. The intersection of quantum computing and cybersecurity is uncharted territory, but by embracing innovation, collaboration, and vigilance, we can navigate the quantum horizon while ensuring the security as well as resilience of the digital future.

CHAPTER XI

Regulatory Compliance and Legal Considerations

GDPR, CCPA, and Other Regulations

In an increasingly digitized world, where data has become a valuable currency, the need for comprehensive data privacy and protection regulations has never been more pressing. As individuals entrust their personal information to many online platforms and services, the risk of data breaches and misuse has escalated, necessitating the establishment of stringent legal frameworks to safeguard user rights. Two prominent examples of such regulations are the GDPR (also known as General Data Protection Regulation) of the European Union and the CCPA (also known as California Consumer Privacy Act) in the United States. This section explores the significance, scope, key provisions, implications, and broader impact of these regulations while highlighting the emergence of similar regulations in other parts of the world.

The GDPR, enacted by the European Union in 2018, and the CCPA, effective in California from 2020, have been instrumental in ushering in a new era of data privacy and protection. These regulations respond to the growing concerns surrounding data breaches, unauthorized data collection, and the lack of transparency in processing personal information. By placing the rights of individuals at the forefront and imposing obligations on organizations that handle personal data, GDPR and CCPA seek to restore user trust and give individuals greater control over their data.

The GDPR's scope extends beyond the borders of the European Union, affecting any organization that processes the personal data of EU citizens. It permits individuals rights such as the right to be informed, the right to access their data, the right to rectify inaccuracies, the right to erasure (also referred to as the "right to be forgotten"), and more. It also requires organizations to acquire explicit consent before processing personal data, mandates data breach notifications, and imposes substantial fines for non-compliance.

The CCPA, on the other hand, primarily applies to organizations that conduct business in California and meet specific revenue and data processing criteria. It grants consumers the right to know what personal information is being collected about them, the right to opt-out of the sale of their data, the right to access their data, and the right to request the deletion of their data. Similar to GDPR, the CCPA also imposes penalties for non-compliance.

The implications of GDPR and CCPA reach far beyond the regions they directly govern. Organizations worldwide that interact with EU citizens or Californian residents must comply with these regulations, leading to a global shift towards more transparent data practices and heightened user privacy. The impact has been felt across industries, leading companies to reassess their data handling practices, implement better data protection measures, and invest in tools and technologies that facilitate compliance.

The influence of GDPR and CCPA has spurred the development of similar data privacy regulations in other parts of the world. Lei Geral de Proteção de Dados (or LGPD) of Brazil and Personal Information Protection and Electronic Documents Act (PIPEDA) of Canada are examples of regulations that align with the principles of user consent, data transparency, and individual rights. Additionally, India's Personal Data Protection Bill is currently under consideration and shares similarities with GDPR and CCPA in its data privacy and protection approach.

Complying with regulations like GDPR and CCPA poses challenges for organizations. The complexity of data ecosystems, the need for robust consent management, and the potential impact on business models are just a few of the considerations. Ensuring the security of stored data, implementing data breach response plans, and creating a culture of data privacy are ongoing efforts.

In an era where data has become a digital currency, regulations such as GDPR, CCPA, and their counterparts worldwide play a pivotal role in safeguarding individual rights and promoting transparent data practices. The significance of these regulations extends beyond geographical boundaries, reshaping the global landscape of data privacy and protection. As technology evolves and data breaches remain a constant threat, the importance of robust data privacy regulations and compliance cannot be overstated. Organizations must continue to adapt their practices to align with these regulations to avoid penalties and cultivate trust, transparency, and accountability in their data handling processes.

Cybersecurity Frameworks (NIST, ISO 27001, etc.)

In an interconnected and digitized world, the importance of cybersecurity cannot be overstated. The relentless evolution of cyber threats demands a structured and adaptable approach to safeguarding digital assets and sensitive information. This is where cybersecurity frameworks come into play. These frameworks provide structured guidelines, best practices, and methodologies to help organizations effectively manage their cybersecurity posture. Among the prominent cybersecurity frameworks, the National Institute of Standards and Technology (or NIST) Cybersecurity Framework and International Organization for Standardization (ISO) 27001 stand out as comprehensive blueprints for addressing cybersecurity challenges. This section explores the significance, scope, key components, benefits, and considerations associated with these frameworks, shedding light on how organizations can enhance their cyber resilience.

The NIST Cybersecurity Framework was introduced by the United States National Institute of Standards and Technology as a response to the escalating cyber threats facing both public and private sectors. It offers a flexible and adaptable approach to managing cybersecurity risk, enabling organizations to align their cybersecurity activities with their business objectives. The framework's core consists of five functions: Identify, Protect, Detect, Respond, and Recover.

ISO 27001 which was developed by the International Organization for Standardization, is a globally acknowledged standard for information security management systems (ISMS). It offers a systematic approach to managing sensitive information, ensuring its confidentiality, integrity, and availability. ISO 27001 defines a structured framework for establishing, implementing, monitoring, maintaining, and improving an

ISMS, encompassing risk assessment, risk treatment, and continual improvement.

Both the NIST Cybersecurity Framework and ISO 27001 share key components that organizations must consider when implementing effective cybersecurity measures. Risk assessment and management lie at the core of both frameworks, requiring organizations to identify and assess vulnerabilities, threats, and impacts. Furthermore, implementing appropriate safeguards to protect assets and sensitive information is critical.

The adoption of cybersecurity frameworks offers a myriad of benefits to organizations. One of the primary advantages is their structured approach, guiding organizations through a step-by-step process of identifying vulnerabilities, mitigating risks, and responding effectively to incidents. These frameworks also enable organizations to establish a common language for discussing cybersecurity risks, fostering collaboration among various departments and stakeholders. Furthermore, adopting recognized frameworks can enhance an organization's credibility and trustworthiness, reassuring customers, partners, and regulators of its commitment to cybersecurity.

Implementing cybersecurity frameworks is challenging. Organizations may face difficulties mapping the frameworks to their business needs and risk profiles. Additionally, achieving full compliance and maintaining alignment with evolving threats can be complex and resource-intensive. The involvement of leadership and commitment at all levels is crucial to successfully implementing and continuously improving these frameworks.

Both the NIST Cybersecurity Framework and ISO 27001 emphasize flexibility and adaptability. This is crucial in the ever-changing landscape of cyber threats. As new threats emerge and technology evolves, organizations must be able to adjust their cybersecurity strategies accordingly. These frameworks provide a solid foundation while allowing organizations to tailor their approaches to their unique needs and risk profiles.

Cyber threats are relentless and ever-evolving in a world where cybersecurity frameworks offer a structured and strategic approach to safeguarding sensitive information, digital assets, and organizational reputation. The NIST Cybersecurity Framework and ISO 27001 are comprehensive blueprints, guiding organizations through identifying risks, implementing safeguards, and responding effectively to incidents. While challenges may arise in implementing and maintaining these frameworks, their benefits in terms of enhanced cybersecurity posture, stakeholder trust, and adaptability to changing threats are substantial. By embracing these frameworks and continually refining their cybersecurity strategies, organizations can navigate the complex landscape of cyber threats with resilience and confidence.

Legal and Financial Consequences of Data Breaches

In today's interconnected digital landscape, data breaches have become a ubiquitous threat, impacting organizations across industries and geographies. Beyond the immediate technological and operational challenges they pose, data breaches carry profound legal and financial consequences that can reverberate long after the breach itself. This section delves into the intricate web of legal and financial implications associated with data breaches, exploring the regulatory landscape, potential legal liabilities, financial losses, and strategies to mitigate these multifaceted impacts.

The regulatory environment surrounding data breaches has evolved significantly in response to the escalating frequency and scale of breaches. Regulations like the GDPR in the European Union and the CCPA in the United States impose stringent requirements on organizations to protect the personal data they collect, process, and store. Failure to adhere with these regulations can result in severe penalties. GDPR, for instance, can impose fines of up to 4% of yearly global turnover or €20 million, whichever is higher, for non-compliance.

Legal liabilities stemming from data breaches extend beyond regulatory fines. Organizations can face lawsuits from individuals affected by the breach, seeking compensation for damages such as identity theft, financial losses, and emotional distress. These lawsuits can be costly and time-consuming, tarnishing an organization's reputation and eroding customer trust.

The financial repercussions of a data breach are multifaceted, ranging from immediate costs to long-term impacts. Tangible costs include expenses associated with breach containment, investigation, and notifying affected individuals. Organizations often need to engage cybersecurity experts, forensic investigators, and legal counsel to assess the extent of the breach, identify vulnerabilities, and devise strategies for recovery.

Furthermore, data breaches can lead to operational disruptions that result in revenue losses. Downtime, loss of customers, and diminished market value can all contribute to substantial financial setbacks. The cost of reputational damage and the resources needed for public relations efforts to restore trust add to the financial burden.

While the financial losses associated with data breaches are quantifiable, the intangible costs can be equally if not more damaging. Reputational damage resulting from a breach can have far-reaching consequences. Loss of customer trust, negative media coverage, and public perception of negligence can lead to decreased customer loyalty and diminished brand value. Rebuilding a tarnished reputation is a challenging and resource-intensive endeavor.

Organizations can proactively mitigate the legal and financial consequences of data breaches. Preparedness is key. Implementing robust cybersecurity measures, encryption protocols, and access controls can reduce the risk of breaches. Developing an incident response plan that outlines roles, responsibilities, and communication strategies is crucial for containing breaches and minimizing their impact.

Cyber insurance is another valuable tool for managing the financial fallout of a breach. These policies can cover costs related to breach response, legal fees, notification efforts, and even potential fines. However, reviewing policy terms and exclusions is essential to ensure comprehensive coverage carefully.

The financial and legal consequences of data breaches underscore the far-reaching impacts of these incidents. In an era where digital data is a critical asset, organizations must navigate a complex landscape of regulations, liabilities, and costs. A comprehensive approach encompassing robust cybersecurity measures, incident response planning, and risk management strategies is essential for mitigating data breaches' legal and financial impacts. As the digital landscape continues to develop, organizations prioritizing data protection and security will be better equipped to navigate the intricate web of legal complexities and financial challenges posed by data breaches while safeguarding their reputation and customer trust.

CHAPTER XII

Building a Cybersecurity Culture

Creating a Security-Focused Organizational Culture

In today's interconnected and digitally-driven world, cybersecurity is no longer a concern relegated to the IT department; it is a critical consideration that permeates every facet of an organization. As cyber threats become more and more sophisticated and prevalent, fostering a security-focused organizational culture has become a strategic imperative. This section delves into the significance of a security-focused culture, explores the key components required to cultivate it, highlights the benefits for both organizations and employees, and discusses the role of leadership in driving this cultural transformation.

A security-focused organizational culture is more than just a set of policies and procedures; it is a mindset that prioritizes cybersecurity in every action and decision. Such a culture recognizes that cybersecurity is not solely the responsibility of the IT department but a collective effort that involves all employees, from top executives to entry-level staff. This cultural shift is imperative due to the escalating frequency and sophistication of cyberattacks that can disrupt operations, compromise sensitive data, and damage an organization's reputation. Creating a security-focused culture requires several key components to be in place. Communication and education are paramount. Employees must understand the importance of cybersecurity, the potential risks they face, and their role in safeguarding the organization. Regular training sessions and workshops can equip employees with the knowledge and skills to identify phishing attempts, protect sensitive information, and respond to security incidents.

Accountability and ownership are also essential elements. Employees should feel responsible for cybersecurity and understand that their actions directly impact the organization's overall security posture. Encouraging open communication and reporting potential security threats without fear of retribution fosters a culture of vigilance and proactivity.

A security-focused organizational culture yields a multitude of benefits. For organizations, it reduces the risk of security breaches and associated costs, including financial losses, regulatory fines, and reputational damage. It enhances customer trust, as clients and partners are more likely to collaborate with organizations that prioritize cybersecurity. A security-focused culture also streamlines compliance efforts, making adhering to regulations and standards easier.

For employees, a security-focused culture empowers them with the knowledge and tools needed to protect their personal information, both at work and in their personal lives. It fosters a sense of pride in contributing to the organization's security and resilience. Additionally, a culture that values cybersecurity can attract and retain top talent, as professionals increasingly seek workplaces that prioritize their digital well-being.

Creating and nurturing a security-focused culture starts at the top. Setting the tone and serving as an example for the rest of the team is leadership. Executives should champion cybersecurity initiatives, actively participate in training sessions, and demonstrate a commitment to best practices. Leadership involvement lends credibility to cybersecurity's importance and motivates employees to follow suit.

Furthermore, leadership must allocate resources and support initiatives that promote cybersecurity awareness. Whether investing in training programs, updating security technologies, or rewarding employees for vigilant behavior, a commitment to cybersecurity should be reflected in organizational priorities and decision-making.

While building a security-focused culture is essential, it's not without its challenges. Resistance to change, lack of awareness, and competing priorities can hinder cultural transformation efforts. Overcoming these challenges requires a long-term commitment, consistent communication, and a phased approach that gradually introduces security measures and practices.

Sustaining the culture is equally important. Regular reinforcement through training, workshops, newsletters, and internal communications is necessary to ensure that cybersecurity remains top of mind for employees. Recognizing and rewarding employees for contributing to a secure environment reinforces the cultural shift and encourages ongoing engagement.

A security-focused organizational culture is more than a buzzword; it's a strategic imperative in an era where cyber threats are pervasive. By fostering a culture that values cybersecurity, organizations can enhance their resilience, protect sensitive information, and build trust with stakeholders. The components of communication, education, accountability, and leadership support are crucial in driving this cultural transformation. As technology evolves and cyber threats become increasingly complex, organizations prioritizing a security-focused culture will be better equipped to explore the ever-changing landscape of cybersecurity with confidence and vigilance.

Collaboration between IT and Non-IT Teams

In the digital age, where organizations operate within a complex web of interconnected systems and data flows, the importance of cybersecurity transcends the realm of IT departments. Cyber threats are no longer limited to technical vulnerabilities; they encompass a wide array of human factors, making it imperative for a cybersecurity culture to extend throughout an organization. The collaborative effort between IT and non-IT teams are pivotal in building a robust cybersecurity culture that is both proactive and resilient. This section delves into the significance of collaboration between these teams, explores the challenges and benefits, highlights strategies for effective communication and cooperation, and emphasizes the role of leadership in fostering this cross-functional partnership.

A cybersecurity culture is not confined to the domain of IT professionals alone; it requires the active participation and commitment of all employees, regardless of their roles. Cyber threats often exploit human vulnerabilities, such as social engineering and phishing attacks, making non-technical staff susceptible targets. Organizations can ensure cybersecurity becomes a shared responsibility and priority by fostering collaboration between IT and non-IT teams.

Collaboration between IT and non-IT teams presents its share of challenges. Communication gaps and differing perspectives can hinder effective cooperation. IT teams might struggle to convey technical concepts to non-IT personnel, while non-IT teams might perceive cybersecurity measures as impediments to their workflow.

However, the benefits of collaboration far outweigh the challenges. A united front enhances the organization's collective defense against cyber threats. Non-IT teams bring domain-specific knowledge that can help IT teams tailor cybersecurity measures to the organization's unique needs. Additionally, non-IT teams can serve as a human firewall by recognizing and reporting potential security incidents, reducing the response time to threats.

Effective collaboration hinges on clear communication and mutual understanding. IT teams must translate technical jargon into accessible language that resonates with non-IT staff. Regular cybersecurity training and awareness programs can bridge the knowledge gap, educating non-IT personnel about best practices, threat vectors, and incident response protocols.

Engaging non-IT teams in the cybersecurity decision-making process is also crucial. Involving them in risk assessments, policy development, and incident response planning strengthens the cybersecurity culture and highlights the organization's commitment to its digital well-being.

Leadership sets the tone for collaboration between IT and non-IT teams. Executives should champion the importance of a cybersecurity culture and establish it as a top-level priority. Their endorsement lends credibility and urgency to the partnership, motivating IT and non-IT teams to participate actively.

Moreover, leadership should allocate resources to cybersecurity initiatives, ensuring both teams have the tools and training they need to succeed. Recognizing and rewarding collaboration reinforces the desired behavior and creates a positive feedback loop.

Collaboration between IT and non-IT teams goes beyond implementing security measures; it's about cultivating a holistic cybersecurity mindset that permeates the organization's DNA. This mindset encompasses an understanding that cybersecurity is not solely the responsibility of the IT department, but a collective effort to safeguard the organization's assets, data, and reputation.

Leadership can facilitate this mindset shift by promoting an environment of openness and trust. Encouraging the reporting of near-misses or suspicious activities, without fear of repercussions, creates a culture of continuous learning and improvement.

Several organizations have successfully harnessed the power of collaboration between IT and non-IT teams to build a strong cybersecurity culture. For example, a financial institution revamped its cybersecurity training program, tailoring it to the specific roles of different departments. This approach empowered employees to apply cybersecurity best practices in their daily tasks, significantly decreasing security incidents.

In another case, a multinational corporation established a cross-functional cybersecurity committee that included representatives from various departments. This committee spearheaded cybersecurity awareness campaigns, assessed risks, and ensured security measures aligned with business needs. The result was a cohesive cybersecurity strategy addressing technical vulnerabilities and human factors.

Building a cybersecurity culture demands collaboration between IT and non-IT teams in an era where cyber threats exploit human vulnerabilities as much as technical weaknesses. The cross-functional partnership enhances an organization's collective defense, enables tailored cybersecurity measures, and empowers non-IT personnel to participate actively in cybersecurity efforts. By bridging communication gaps, involving non-IT teams in decision-making, and promoting a holistic cybersecurity mindset, organizations can foster a culture where cybersecurity is not a departmental concern but a shared responsibility. Through effective collaboration and a commitment to cybersecurity, organizations can build resilience, protect their assets, and navigate the evolving landscape of cyber threats with confidence and unity.

Continual Learning and Adaptation

Building a strong cybersecurity culture has become a strategic imperative for organizations in the ever-evolving digital landscape, where cyber threats constantly mutate and adapt. However, achieving cybersecurity excellence is not a one-time effort; it requires a commitment to continual learning and adaptation. This section explores the significance of ongoing education in fostering a cybersecurity culture, delves into the key components of a learning-focused approach, highlights the benefits for organizations and employees, and discusses strategies for embedding a culture of continuous improvement.

As cyber threats rise in complexity and sophistication, organizations can no longer rely on static security measures to protect their digital assets. Cyber attackers are adept at finding new vulnerabilities, necessitating a dynamic and adaptive cybersecurity culture. Continual learning is at the heart of this culture, enabling employees to stay up-to-date with the latest threats, technologies, and best practices. Without ongoing education, an organization's cybersecurity practices can quickly become obsolete, leaving them vulnerable to emerging risks.

A learning-focused approach to cybersecurity culture entails several key components. Regular cybersecurity training is paramount, ensuring that employees have the knowledge and skills to determine and respond to threats. These training sessions should cover a variety of topics, from phishing awareness to secure coding practices, tailored to different teams' specific roles and responsibilities.

Additionally, organizations should promote a culture of curiosity and learning. Encouraging employees to stay informed about cybersecurity trends, attend industry conferences, and engage in online forums fosters a sense of ownership and vigilance. Furthermore, a robust incident response plan that includes post-incident analysis and lessons learned is essential for continuous improvement.

The benefits of a continual learning approach to cybersecurity culture are far-reaching. For organizations, ongoing education enhances their ability to anticipate and mitigate threats, reducing the risk of breaches and associated costs. It fosters a culture of proactive security, where employees actively contribute to the organization's defense against cyber threats. This, in turn, enhances the organization's reputation and customer trust.

For employees, continual learning equips them with valuable skills that can improve their career prospects and empowers them to protect their personal information and digital presence. A culture of learning and cybersecurity awareness contributes to a sense of job satisfaction and pride in contributing to the organization's security posture.

Embedding a culture of continuous improvement requires a multifaceted approach. Regularly scheduled cybersecurity training sessions should be complemented by microlearning opportunities, such as informative videos, quizzes, and infographics, that can be accessed on-demand. This accommodates different learning styles and ensures that cybersecurity remains a part of employees' daily routine.

Engagement and gamification can also play a role in fostering continual learning. Implementing friendly competitions, rewards, and recognition for employees who excel in cybersecurity awareness or reporting potential threats can make the learning process engaging and motivating.

Leadership sets the tone for a learning-focused cybersecurity culture. Executives should champion and prioritize ongoing education by allocating resources, endorsing training initiatives, and participating in training themselves. When leadership actively engages in learning, it communicates the importance of cybersecurity across all levels of the organization.

Moreover, leadership should foster an environment where learning is valued and mistakes are seen as opportunities for improvement. Encouraging employees to report near-misses or incidents without fear of retribution creates a culture of transparency and a shared commitment to cybersecurity excellence.

Several organizations have reaped the benefits of embedding a culture of continuous learning in their cybersecurity efforts. For instance, a technology company implemented regular "Lunch and Learn" sessions, where cybersecurity experts shared insights, trends, and practical tips with employees. This approach increased cybersecurity awareness and fostered a sense of community and collaboration among employees.

In another case, a healthcare institution introduced a gamified training platform that allowed employees to compete in cybersecurity challenges and quizzes. The platform tracked employees' progress and rewarded those who consistently engaged in learning activities. This approach transformed cybersecurity training from a mandatory chore to an engaging and rewarding experience.

Building a robust cybersecurity culture requires a commitment to continual learning and adaptation in a dynamic digital landscape where cyber threats evolve at an unprecedented pace. A learning-focused approach equips employees with the knowledge and skills to identify, mitigate, and respond to emerging threats. This approach benefits organizations by reducing the risk of breaches and enhancing their reputation, empowering employees to protect their digital presence. Embedding a culture of continuous improvement demands leadership endorsement, a diverse range of training methods, and a commitment to transparency and openness. By fostering a cybersecurity culture that embraces ongoing education, organizations can navigate the evolving cyber threat landscape with resilience, confidence, and an unwavering commitment to digital security.

CONCLUSION

Recap of Key Takeaways

As we journey through the pages of this book, "A Journey into Cybersecurity: Mastering Cybersecurity - Expert Insights and Best Practices," we have explored the multifaceted landscape of cybersecurity, delving into its various dimensions, challenges, and strategies. From understanding the foundational concepts to exploring advanced techniques, each chapter has contributed to a comprehensive understanding of navigating the complex realm of digital security. As we recap the key takeaways from each section, we consolidate the insights gained and reinforce the principles that underpin effective cybersecurity practices.

In the initial chapters, we established a strong foundation by exploring the essence of cybersecurity. We recognized that cybersecurity is not merely about technology but a holistic approach that encompasses people, processes, and technology. The CIA triad (Confidentiality, Integrity, and Availability) emerged as a cornerstone, reminding us of the fundamental goals of cybersecurity: preserving data confidentiality, ensuring data integrity, and maintaining system availability.

Moving forward, we explored the strategies that fortify the digital landscape against threats. The Defense in Depth strategy reiterated that relying on a single layer of defense is insufficient. Instead, adopting multiple layers of security ensures that if one layer fails, others remain resilient. Least Privilege and Role-Based Access Control emerged as vital concepts, advocating for restricting access to the minimum necessary for each user or role, thus minimizing potential damage from breaches.

The chapters on threats, attacks, and mitigation strategies were enlightening. From the intricate techniques of social engineering attacks like phishing to insidious insider threats, we recognized that understanding the human element is as crucial as securing technology. Implementing User Awareness and Training emerged as a powerful tool in this regard, as educating users can mitigate the danger of being a victim to social engineering attacks.

Our exploration of technological safeguards, such as Firewalls, Intrusion Detection Systems, and Virtual Private Networks (or VPNs), shed light on how organizations can leverage technology to bolster security. Network Segmentation and Isolation emerged as essential tactics to minimize the lateral movement of threats within networks, ensuring that even if one segment is breached, the entire network is not compromised.

The significance of data encryption was underscored in our discussion of Encryption Algorithms and Methods. We learned that encryption is not merely about protecting data at rest or in transit but also about securing communications and ensuring that only authorized parties can access sensitive information.

Cloud Computing Basics were demystified as the digital landscape evolves, highlighting the shared responsibility model and cloud security best practices. We recognized that while the cloud offers flexibility and scalability, it requires a collaborative effort between cloud service providers and users to ensure robust security.

In our exploration of Common Application Vulnerabilities, we understood that securing applications goes beyond writing code. It involves meticulous testing, adhering to secure coding practices, and continuous monitoring to prevent breaches stemming from vulnerabilities like SQL injection and Cross-Site Scripting (XSS).

Finally, we delved into the Secure Development Lifecycle (SDLC), recognizing that security must be woven into the very fabric of software development. This comprehensive approach ensures that security considerations are integrated from the initial planning stages to deployment and maintenance, reducing the risk of post-development vulnerabilities.

As we reflect on the journey through this book, we recognize that cybersecurity is not a static destination but a dynamic voyage. It demands continuous learning, adaptation, and vigilance. Each chapter has contributed a piece to the intricate puzzle of cybersecurity, equipping us with a toolkit of insights, strategies, and best practices. From the principles of the CIA triad to the intricacies of encryption algorithms, from the complexities of application vulnerabilities to the strategies for securing the development lifecycle, we have uncovered a wealth of knowledge that empowers us to be guardians of the digital realm.

Cybersecurity is one of constant change, as threats evolve and technology advances. Our understanding today serves as a stepping stone for the challenges ahead. By embracing these key takeaways and applying them in our endeavors, we not only bolster our own security but also contribute to the collective resilience of the digital ecosystem. As we bid farewell to this book, let us carry forward these insights, recognizing that our commitment to cybersecurity is a commitment to a safer, more secure digital world.

Encouragement to Prioritize Cybersecurity

In an era where our lives are increasingly intertwined with the digital realm, the importance of cybersecurity cannot be overstated. From personal communications and financial transactions to critical infrastructure and national security, digital systems' integrity, confidentiality, and availability underpin our modern way of life. In this section, we delve into the compelling reasons why individuals, organizations, and governments must prioritize cybersecurity, and how doing so protects our present and secures our digital future.

The digital landscape is rife with threats that have the potential to disrupt, damage, and compromise our digital infrastructure. Cyberattacks, ranging from ransomware to sophisticated nation-state intrusions, have become a ubiquitous concern. The emergence of the Internet of Things (IoT) has further expanded the attack surface, as even everyday devices are connected to the internet. These threats transcend borders, impacting individuals, businesses, and governments globally. As we witness the exponential growth of cybercrime, it becomes evident that cybersecurity is no longer a choice—it's a necessity.

Amid the complex algorithms and cutting-edge technologies, it's essential to recognize that the human element plays a pivotal role in cybersecurity. Most successful cyberattacks exploit human vulnerabilities through tactics like social engineering and phishing. However, education and awareness can empower individuals to become the first line of defense. By promoting a culture of cybersecurity awareness, organizations can equip their employees to recognize and thwart potential threats. Prioritizing cybersecurity education ensures that users understand the risks and contribute to a safer digital environment.

Beyond the immediate threat of attacks, a security breach's economic and reputational consequences can be devastating. For businesses, losing sensitive data or prolonged downtime due to a cyber incident can lead to financial losses, legal liabilities, and erosion of customer trust. The ripple effect extends to supply chains and partners, amplifying the impact. In the digital age, a single breach can tarnish a company's reputation and result in lasting damage. Governments also face similar risks, as attacks on critical infrastructure can disrupt essential services and compromise national security. The financial and reputational toll underscores the need to prioritize cybersecurity as an investment rather than an expense.

Governments worldwide recognize cybersecurity's urgency and enact regulations to ensure a baseline of security practices. Regulatory frameworks such as the European Union's GDPR and the CCPA mandate data protection measures and stipulate penalties for non-compliance. These regulations protect individuals' rights and serve as a wake-up call for organizations to secure their digital assets. Adhering to regulatory standards avoids legal repercussions and demonstrates a commitment to ethical practices and user trust.

As the digital landscape evolves, innovation goes hand in hand with cybersecurity. New technologies, such as AI and blockchain, offer novel ways to enhance security. However, these innovations should be integrated with security considerations from their inception. Collaboration between industries, governments, academia, and cybersecurity experts is crucial for staying ahead of threats. Threat intelligence sharing, best practices, and lessons learned fosters a collective defense mechanism that benefits all stakeholders. Prioritizing cybersecurity as a collaborative effort ensures that the digital future is fortified against emerging threats.

The responsibility of prioritizing cybersecurity extends to the next generation. Educators and educational institutions play a pivotal role in nurturing a future workforce equipped with cybersecurity skills. Incorporating cybersecurity education into curricula equips students with the knowledge to become digital guardians. As technology becomes increasingly integrated into various fields, cybersecurity awareness becomes a universal skill that empowers individuals to protect their personal information and the systems they interact with. By cultivating a generation that understands and values cybersecurity, we lay the groundwork for a safer digital future.

The call to prioritize cybersecurity resonates with urgency in a world where digital threats are dynamic and pervasive. Whether an individual using a smartphone, a small business owner managing customer data, or a government safeguarding critical infrastructure, cybersecurity is a shared responsibility. The risks are too great, the consequences too severe to ignore. By embracing cybersecurity as a fundamental principle, we ensure that the digital landscape remains a space of innovation, communication, and progress. This is not merely a technical challenge; it's a societal imperative. As we navigate the complexities of the digital age, let us prioritize cybersecurity, safeguarding our present and securing a resilient and thriving digital future for future generations.

Looking Ahead to the Future of Cybersecurity

Cybersecurity stands poised for transformative evolution as we stand at the precipice of technological advancement. The digital age has brought unprecedented connectivity and convenience, but it has also ushered in a new era of cyber threats that challenge our ability to protect our digital assets. In this section, we peer into the future of cybersecurity, exploring the trends, challenges, and innovations that will shape the landscape. From the rise of artificial intelligence to the complexities of quantum computing, we unravel the tapestry of possibilities that await and the strategies needed to navigate the dynamic cybersecurity horizon.

A shift in the nature and sophistication of threats marks the future of cybersecurity. As traditional attack vectors continue to be refined, new avenues of attack are also being explored. The generation of connected devices in the Internet of Things (IoT) has opened up a vast attack surface, with attackers targeting smart homes, wearables, and critical infrastructure. With the emergence of 5G technology, the speed and scale of data exchange will escalate, necessitating robust security measures to counteract potential threats. As artificial intelligence (AI) becomes more integrated into everyday life, it also offers new possibilities for defenders and adversaries, with AI-driven attacks and defenses poised to become a defining feature of the cybersecurity landscape.

Integrating AI and machine learning holds immense promise for the future of cybersecurity. AI-driven tools can analyze huge amounts of data, detecting anomalies and patterns that human operators might miss. Machine learning algorithms can enhance threat detection, identify zero-day vulnerabilities, and automate incident response. However, cybercriminals can also exploit this technology to orchestrate more sophisticated attacks. Adversarial machine learning, where attackers manipulate AI algorithms to bypass defenses, poses a significant challenge. Thus, while AI can be a potent ally, its responsible development and deployment are paramount to prevent it from becoming a double-edged sword.

As quantum computing comes closer to becoming a reality, it presents both opportunities and challenges for cybersecurity. Quantum computers have the potential to break currently used encryption algorithms, rendering many existing cryptographic methods obsolete. This underscores the need to develop quantum-resistant encryption techniques to ensure the security of data in the post-quantum era. Simultaneously, quantum technologies offer new cryptographic approaches that can enhance security. Quantum key distribution, for instance, allows for secure communication through the principles of quantum mechanics. Preparing for the advent of quantum computing requires proactive research, collaboration, and standardization efforts to establish a secure foundation for the future.

Amid the technological advancements and digital transformations, the human element remains central to cybersecurity. As attackers increasingly target individuals through social engineering, user awareness and education become paramount. Organizations must foster a cybersecurity culture that empowers employees to identify and report potential threats. Moreover, the shortage of skilled cybersecurity professionals continues to be a challenge. Education and training programs need to be expanded to bridge this gap, and diversity within the field should be encouraged. Empowering individuals to become an active participants in their digital security is a defense mechanism and a societal responsibility.

As the global nature of cyber threats becomes more pronounced, international cooperation is essential. Governments and organizations worldwide must collaborate on establishing cyberspace norms and regulations. Cybersecurity standards and frameworks should transcend borders, ensuring a consistent and unified approach to securing digital infrastructure. Establishing international agreements on cybersecurity best practices, incident response, and information sharing can pave the way for a safer and more interconnected digital world.

As we gaze into the future of cybersecurity, we are met with a blend of optimism and caution. The landscape will undoubtedly be shaped by technological innovation, but it will also be influenced by the decisions we make today. Adapting to emerging threats, harnessing the potential of AI and quantum technologies, nurturing human expertise, and fostering global collaboration are the pillars that will fortify our digital future. As we navigate this dynamic terrain, we must remain vigilant, proactive, and resilient in the face of evolving challenges. The future of cybersecurity is not solely a technical endeavor—it's a collective commitment to safeguarding the digital landscape for generations to come. Through collaboration, innovation, and a dedication to ethical and responsible practices, we can shape a future where the benefits of technology are harnessed without compromising security, privacy, and trust.

Thank you for buying and reading/ listening to our book. If you found this book useful/ helpful please take a few minutes and leave a review on the platform where you purchased our book. Your feedback matters greatly to us.